Legal Almanac Series No. 52

LEGAL PROTECTION FOR THE CONSUMER

by STANLEY MORGANSTERN

This Legal Almanac has been revised by the Oceana Editorial Staff

Irving J. Sloan
General Editor

SECOND EDITION

1978 Oceana Publications, Inc.
Dobbs Ferry, New York

Library of Congress Cataloging in Publication Data

Morganstern, Stanley, 1941-
    Legal protection for the consumer.

    (Legal almanac series; no. 52)
    Includes index.
    1. Consumer protection—Law and legislation—
United States. I. Title.
KF1610.M65   1978   343'.73'07   78-9170
ISBN 0-379-11117-9

© Copyright 1978 by Oceana Publications, Inc.

Manufactured in the United States of America

TABLE OF CONTENTS

iii

INTRODUCTION

"The consumer is moving forward. We cannot rest content until he is in the front row, not displacing the interest of the producer, yet gaining equal rank in representation with that interest. What is new is the concern for the total interest of the consumer, a recognition of certain basic consumer rights: The right to safety, the right to be informed, the right to choose, the right to be hear." President Johnson (1964)

These words of President Johnson have set the tenor of consumerism for the 1970's. The old adage of <u>caveat</u> <u>emptor</u>, let the buyer beware, no longer applies to consumer transactions. To the contrary, the seller is now the one who must beware, and the future will bring an even further swing of the pendulum from favoring the seller to favoring the buyer.

Both the federal government and the state and local governments have worked diligently in promoting the consumer. The number of agencies whose function is to aid the buyer is becoming endless. Legislative enactments aimed at protecting the consumer are increasing each year and cover such varied areas as home remodeling and sale of brewery products.

This almanac is an attempt to aquaint the consumer with those agencies, federal and state, which can aid him. It is an introduction to the vast area of legislation seeking to protect him and assist him in obtaining legal remedies when a seller has mistreated him.

The basis of this almanac is derived primarily from publications obtained from various state agencies which freely disseminate such information upon request. This author gratefully acknowledges the help and assistance of those agencies in preparing this almanac, and has included herein as an appendix a partial listing of agencies available to the consumer seeking help.

The typical objectives of such agencies are as follows:

"To educate and inform the public in order to to make more sophisticated consumers; To process and resolve complaints and inquiries regarding consumer transactions; To do in-depth analysis of specific industries which may need more regulation." (Department of Commerce, Consumer Protection Division, State of Ohio.)

There are approximately thirty-seven states which have enacted legislation seeking to control, eliminate and punish deceptive acts and practices by sellers. Most of these states have appropriated money and manpower to enforce these acts. These agencies and the laws which they seek to enforce cannot, however, be effective unless the consumer is aware of their existance and takes advantage of the services offered.

It is interesting to note that the information supplied by these agencies is primarily directed at educating the consumer. Its message is preventive consumerism, rather than corrective. But an important function of these agencies is to correct problems that have arisen. Corrective methods include mediation, legislation and judicial action.

Areas of consumer education which are the subject of legislation include but are not limited to: buying and servicing new or used cars; borrowing, buying or building a new home; arranging or financing funerals; home appliances; insurance; real estate promotions; jewelry; home furnishing; moving and storage; utilities and transportation; guarantees; foods and drugs; false advertising; professional services; finance companies; repair services; door-to-door sales; franchises; travel agencies; magazine subscriptions; mobile homes and many others.

The President's Advisory Council on Consumer Affairs has established goals for successful consumer education:

1.   A rudimentary understanding of a market economy and the consumer's position in it, particularly his responsibility to make intelligent choices,

2.   Knowledge of standards of quality and an ability to translate the technical jargon often used by manufacturers and advertisers into everyday language,

3.   Knowledge of sources of information about products,

4.   Knowledge of existing legislation and regulatory agencies that serve consumers,

5.   An alertness toward fraudulent and misleading advertising and all other fraudulent schemes,

6. General understanding of the legal rights and recourse of consumers,

7. Knowledge of certain goods and services and what features to look for when making buying decisions.

Of course this almanac cannot cover all of the problems in each of these areas, but it will present some case histories provided by the various state agencies. These histories are illustrative of typical problems and how they are solved.

The educational aspect of the various consumer protection divisions cannot be over emphasized. Many of the agencies have employed such diverse means as preparing curriculum and course material for use in schools, both on an adult and student level, radio and television spots, speakers for community and social groups, and mailings of educational material.

The scope of consumer protection activities in Michigan was described by Frank J. Kelly, Attorney General:

"It has been our endeavor to mobilize the resources of law enforcement agencies, business organizations, service clubs, labor organizations and other public and private clubs in the war against consumer frauds. We have initiated legislation, fought successful civil law suits, brought criminal actions against individuals and organizations, engaged in educational programs and taken other actions designed to make Michigan an unpleasant place for consumer fraud activities."

These activities are typical of the efforts of consumer divisions throughout the United States. To explore each of the divisions and the legislative enactments would require several volumes, but we shall present the most typical statutes and explore in some detail the ways and means by which a consumer can prevent and correct consumer frauds in many areas. These include not only direct frauds by misrepresentations of price, quality, warranties and the like, but also deceptive advertising practices, home soliciations, and all other areas where the consumer is at the mercy of the seller.

Chapter I
CONSUMER
PROTECTION: FEDERAL

The Federal Trade Commission (FTC)

The Federal Trade Commission is the major federal agency dealing with consumer protection problems. Its authority extends to conduct in interstate commerce. It administers the Federal Trade Commission Act, the Wool Labeling Act, the Trademark Act, the Fur Products Labeling Act, and the Textile Fiber Identification Act. The FTC also enforces the Fair Packaging and Labeling Act, which prohibits unfair and deceptive packaging and labeling of any consumer commodity shipped in interstate commerce, and the Truth in Lending Act which controls the finance charges on loans and regulates what must be disclosed in a loan. The Act provides for private as well as public enforcement of the disclosure provisions. Private citizens may recover twice the amount of the finance charge in connection with the transaction, up to a maximum of $1,000. The successful plaintiff can additionally recover court costs and reasonable attorney's fees. The Truth in Lending Act also limits the liability of a credit card holder to only $50 for the unauthorized use of the card by another person. Even this liability may be waived if the issuer of the card does not provide a self-addressed pre-stamped notification to be mailed in the event of loss or theft of the credit card, and if the issuer does not provide a method to identify the user of the card as an authorized user, such as an electronic confirmation.

In addition, the FTC enforces the Consumer Credit Reporting Act. This Act restricts the release of a credit report on a consumer to specified persons for specific reasons. It prohibits obsolete information from being included in the report and restricts who and under what circumstances a person may procure an investigative report on any consumer. The Act compels disclosure of credit report information to the affected consumer upon request.

The FTC enforces all of these acts through a number of local offices.* Its powers include both rulemaking and issuance of (voluntary) industry guides to comply with the regulations. For example, recent guidelines issued include: auto pricing practices, credit card billing, unsolicited credit cards, door to door sales (cooling off period), retail food ads, and unsolicited merchandise.

The FTC has exercised some control over franchise arrangements which have involved unfair trade practices, such as overstating a prospective franchise's sales volume.

In its enforcement activities, the FTC has occasions to consider revising some of its rule in light of current methods and practices and is almost always considering new areas of regulation.

The Food and Drug Administration (FDA)

The FDA in the Department of Health, Education and Welfare is primarily responsible for administering the federal Food, Drug and Cosmetic Act. Section 331 of this Act is the heart of the protection afforded consumers. It prohibits the introduction into interstate commerce of adulterated or misbranded goods. It also prohibits alteration or removal of any label of a food, drug or cosmetic while such article is held for sale after shipment in interstate commerce. To effectuate the directives of this Act, the agency has adopted extensive regulations for control of food, food additives, drugs and cosmetics.

Pursuant to this Act, the FDA has launched into the regulation of many other consumer protection areas, including: the use of prescription drugs for conditions not named in the official labeling; food labeling; a review of all over the counter drugs currently marketed; labeling rules on dietary foods, imitation foods and frozen desserts; registration of blood banks; and the filing of cosmetic products and raw material composition statements.

---

* Regional offices are located in Atlanta, Boston, Chicago, Cleveland, Kansas City, Los Angeles, New Orleans, New York City, San Francisco and Seattle. The FTC's Bureau of Consumer Protection is at Sixth & Pennsylvania Avenue, Washington, D.C. 20580. Office of Information at same address.

The FDA also administers the Caustic Poisons Act which prohibits shipment in interstate commerce of misbranded, dangerous, caustic or corrosive substances, and the Import Mil Act.

The Department of Agriculture

The Department of Agriculture administers the Wholesome Poultry Products Act (Poultry Products Inspection Act), the Federal Meat Inspection Act (Wholesome Meat Act), the Egg Products Inspection Act, the Perishable Agricultural Commodities Act, the Agricultural Marketing Act, and the Packers and Stockyards Act, each of which affects the quality of food available to the consumer.

The Postal Service

The United States Postal Service administers the postal fraud statutes which prohibit the use of the mails for fraudulent purposes, allow the postmaster to stop receipt of mail by the person by returning the mail with the marking "fraudulent", and permit temporary impounding of mail. These laws, which together have been termed "a powerful consumer protection law," can potentially curb fraudulent practices in mail order sales.

The Department of Housing and Urban Development (HUD)

HUD administers the Interstate Land Sales Full Disclosure Act which requires the registration of subdivisions and filing of a statement when an interstate land sale is involved. This statement is aimed at the disclosure of such features of that particular parcel of land as ownership, title problems, physical accessibility, safety hazards, public utility access, easements and encumbrances.

The Consumer Product Safety Commission (CPSC)

The Consumer Product Safety Commission represents a major effort to protect consumers against unreasonable risks of personal injury and to help consumers evaluate the comparative safety of products. The Commission is armed with comprehensive authority to set safety standards, ban products that cannot

3

be made safe, rid the market of imminently hazardous products, require record keeping, examine records, call for reports, inspect business premises, require labeling, warning, and instructional information directions, and demand safety certifications. The enabling legislation for CPSC also contains provisions covering defect notices, recalls, replacements, repairs, purchase price refunds, information collection and publication, new products, exports and imports. These requirements are backed up by enforcement devices -- civil and criminal penalties, injunctions, seizures, condemnations, import exclusions and consumer suits.

Besides this extensive general authority, the CPSC has assumed the functions of the FDA under the Hazardous Substances Act and the Poison Prevention Packaging Act, as well as the functions of the FTC and the Department of Commerce in administering the Flammable Fabrics Act.

Office of Consumer Affairs (OCA)

The President by Executive Order 11583 in February, 1971, established an Office of Consumer Affairs in the Executive Office of the President. The Office is now part of the Department of Health, Education and Welfare. The objectives of the Office of Consumer Affairs include co-ordinating federal consumer programs, advising the President and federal agencies on policies and plans as they affect the consumer interest, recommending legislation and encouraging and coordinating research and consumer programs.*

Other Federal Laws

Other federal laws have been passed to aid the consumer. For example, extortionate credit transactions are prohibited. The Federal Reserve Board may regulate, license or prohibit certain credit transactions under the Federal Credit Control Act. Federal restrictions on wage garnishment have also been enacted. Title III of the Consumer Credit Protection Act of 1968 restricts the amount of garnishable earnings to 25% of the

----

* The Office of Consumer Affairs is located in the New Executive Office Building, Room 6025, Washington, D.C. 20506.

debtor's disposable earnings in any given week and prohibit an employer from discharging any employee because his earnings have been subjected to garnishment for any one indebtedness.

One of the most effective weapons in the consumer protection arsenal, the class action, was considerably weakened by a 1975 U.S. Supreme Court case, Eisen v. Carlisle & Jacquelin. That case held that individual notice must be sent to each class member whose name and address could be ascertained through reasonable effort, regardless of the possibly prohibitive cost this would entail for the representative plaintiff. Over 2,250,000 class members were involved in the case. Thus, the effective use of the class action by consumer protection groups has greatly diminished.

Federal Consumer Agency Legislation

Federal consumer representation legislation has been proposed from time to time during the past several decades. Proposals were introduced in the Senate in 1929 and in 1932 to create a "consumer counsel." The 1929 proposal was defeated, and in 1932 President Hoover vetoed the bill to which the consumer proposal was an amendment.

The consumer movement gained momentum after 1933, but proposals by President Franklin D. Roosevelt nevertheless never got off the ground. The creation of a cabinet-level Consumer Department was proposed during the late 1930's, but it was not until 1959 that consumer legislation first appeared in Congress. The late Senator Estes Kefauver and twenty-one cosponsors introduced a bill to create a cabinet level Department of Consumers.

In March 1962, President John F. Kennedy issued the first Presidential message to Congress addressing consumer interests. He also created a consumer advisory council within the Council of Economic Advisers. But the Council existed for only eighteen months, never meeting again after making its first report in October 1963.

In January 1964 President Lyndon B. Johnson issued an executive order creating the President's Committee on Consumer Interests.

During the 91st Congress (1969-70) there were five related consumer-representation concepts before Congress. A compromise bill calling for an independent consumer protection agency

5

and a council of consumer advisors in the White House passed the Senate, but failed in the House Rules Committee. In 1971 legislation to establish an independent consumer protection agency with far weaker powers than in the Senate-passed 1970 bill was adopted by the House, but died in the Senate. The measure had been endorsed by Virginia Knauser, the President's special assistant for consumer affairs, but denounced by Ralph Nader, who was in favor of giving the agency stronger advocacy powers.

As a result, action in both houses demonstrated a shift away from cabinet-level department proposals, and the independent consumer agency concept emerged from the Government Operations committees of both houses as the recommended approach with its consumer advocacy function, only one feature of leading consumer department bills, as the dominant feature.

In 1971 President Richard Nixon by executive order enlarged the existing White House Consumer Advisor Office and asked Congress to delay action on an independent agency.

In the 92nd Congress (1971-72), Senators Ribicoff, Javits and Percy introduced a bill which would have created a stronger consumer agency than those proposed in previous bills. The bill failed as a result of a filibuster, although a weaker bill had passed the House.

Two major bills were considered in the 93rd Congress in 1973 by Senator Ribicoff. While Virginia Knauser, the President's chief spokesman on consumer affairs, endorsed the bill in principle, President Nixon threatened to veto it if passed in the form in which it was proposed. The bill was fiercely debated in each chamber in 1974, and, although the proposal passed the House, the Senate bill was tabled after four attempts at cloture. Senator Ribicoff continued to introduce such bills in 1975, 1976, and in 1977. Congress failed to pass the last attempt in 1977.

The proposed Consumer Protection Act of 1977 would have established an independent, nonregulatory Agency for Consumer Advocacy, with authority to represent the interests of consumers before federal agencies and the courts. The agency would be administered by a presidential appointee for a term coterminous with that of the President, but not to exceed four years. Its defeat in 1977 does not mean the end of such legislation. Sooner or later its time will come.

6

Chapter II
SELECTED STATE LEGISLATION

Since there is at the present time no standard uniform state law covering the various areas of consumerism, it is necessary to examine at least a few of the individual state laws. Generally, these acts cover a wide variety of consumer problems and punish the sellers or advertisers who commit practices in violation of the laws. These acts may be called deceptive trade practices and deceptive advertising acts. Many states combine the two main areas into a single law while others have enacted separate and distinct laws on each subject.

The enforcement of the laws is generally vested in the state attorney general's office, who, with the aid of investigatory powers and the courts, prosecutes the vendors who have violated any provision of the acts. Most of the state laws, while often providing severe civil and criminal penalties, do not abrogate the consumer's right to bring a private lawsuit. Many, in fact, provide explicitly for such suits and dicatate the awarding of double or triple damages along with costs of suit and attorney fees.

While it is not possible to review thoroughly each of the states and each of the state enactments, we shall summarize the consumer legislation of many states. The reader should be aware, however, that an in-depth study of the particular statute in question should be made before seeking to apply it to his particular situation. Appendix A in this volume contains the statutors references to each state's consumer protection laws.

ALASKA

In 1970 Alaska enacted an Unfair Trade Practices and Consumer Protection Act. Under that act the following practices are unlawful:

> 1. To fraudulently convey or transfer goods or services by representing them to be those of another;
>
> 2. To falsely represent or designate the geographic origin of any goods or services;

7

3. To cause possible confusion as to the source, sponsorship, approval, affiliation or association with or certification of goods or services, or to actually misrepresent such approval, sponsorship, etc;

4. To represent used goods as new;

5. To misrepresent the quality of goods or services;

6. To disparage the goods and services of another by false or misleading representations;

7. To advertise goods or services with the intent not to sell them as advertised;

8. To mislead by advertising that goods are available for sale when in fact there are not enough of such goods to supply a reasonable demand;

9. To mislead as to the reasons for, existence of, or amounts of, price reductions;

10. To engage in any other conduct which would damage a buyer or competitor;

11. To employ deceptive practices, fraud, false pretense or the like in the sale or advertisement of goods and services whether or not any person has actually been mislead, deceived or damaged;

12. To fail to meet the disclosure provisions of the act as to installment sales contracts.

Although the Alaska statute appears to be most thorough in its inclusion of possible deceptive practices, other acts done by vendors, though not included in the codified law, may be subject to civil lawsuits brought under traditional common law principles. Criminal prosecutions arise from intentional and knowing violations of the statute.

Since the act includes advertising provisions, the typical exemptions are found. Owners and publishers of newspapers, and television and radio station owners and operators are excluded so long as there is no knowing participation in the unlawful act. Likewise, advertisements governed by other federal and state statutes do not fall within the application of this particular statute.

The attorney general of the state is authorized to investigate alleged violations of the act, to prosecute offenders and to obtain injunctions. The courts can return monies or property to the consumer who has been damaged by reason of the unlawful act. Written assurances of future compliance may be obtained.

The act specifically authorizes private or class actions by consumers. The courts in such actions may award the consumer his actual damages or two hundred dollars, whichever is greater. Willful violations of the act, proved in a civil suit, may result in treble damages or equitable relief if warranted.

Interestingly, the Alaska statute is unique in that it requires the plaintiffs in a class action to post a bond in the sum of five thousand dollars. In the event the plaintiffs do not prevail in the litigation, the bond may be used to cover the defendant's costs and attorney fees incurred in defending the suit. Many statutes allow the plaintiff to recover attorney fees in such suits, but do not give parity to the defendants if they are successful. This one does just that and appears to be most equitable.

A civil action may be commenced within two years from the time the consumer discovers, or reasonably should have discovered, his loss.

Another interesting provision of this statute makes manufacturers or suppliers of merchandise which is the basis for the action liable for the damages assessed to, or suffered by retailers charged under the statute. Penalties for violation of the provisions of the statute are, as in many other states, rather severe. A violation of an injunction can result in a fine up to twenty-five thousand dollars for each and every violation. Other violations of the statute may cost the offender from five to ten thousand dollars.

ARIZONA

The Division of Consumer Fraud was created in the state of Arizona in 1966. That division is aided by state legislation which makes unlawful any practice, fraud, misrepresentation or the like, employed in consumer transactions. Likewise, the omission of any material fact in the advertising of goods and services is an unlawful act under the Arizona statute.

An act or omission may be unlawful despite the fact that

the consumer has not actually been misled or damaged by the misrepresentation. The deceptive act or omission in and of itself is all that is necessary to constitute an unlawful act.

Any advertisement which amounts to an attempt to induce a person to enter into any obligation or acquire any title or interest in any merchandise is covered and regulated by the statute. Such advertisement may be by publication, solicitation or any writing. As in most other statutes regulating advertising, owners of newspapers, publishers, and owners and operators of television and radio stations are exempt from the Arizona statute. In addition, all advertisements subject to or in compliance with the rules and regulations of the Federal Trade Commission are exempt from the operation of this particular statute.

The attorney general of Arizona is empowered to investigate verified written complaints. He may require the charged party to file a written statement concerning the transaction complained of. He may examine, under oath, persons connected with the transaction, and may examine the merchandise, samples thereof, as well as any pertinent books and records of the seller charged with violating the state statutes governing consumer protection.

Once a violation is detected by the attorney general, he is empowered to seek and obtain an injunction. This judicial restraint on activities prohibits the vendor from continuing practices which violate the particular sections of the consumer protection act he has already violated. The courts of Arizona may restore to the injured consumer all monies or property, real or personal, which were lost as a result of the unlawful practice by the vendor. The court may go so far as to appoint a receiver whose function is to make sure the funds or property are returned to the injured consumer.

Since the prime purpose of this type of state consumer protection statute is to assure that violations once found will not recur, the attorney general is authorized to have the violater execute a written statement of future compliance. This written statement is to be filed with the court and strictly complied with by the seller who has signed such.

If any person violates the terms of an injunction or court order, he is subject to a maximum fine of ten thousand dollars. Any person who willfully and intentionally violates any provision of the Arizona statute and is convicted therefore is guilty of a criminal misdemeanor and subject to imprisionment of up to six months and a fine of up to ten thousand dollars, or both.

While the statute contains criminal or monetary civil

penalties, it does not bar a civil suit brought by the aggrieved consumer in his own name. In all actions prosecuted by the attorney general, the guilty party may be required to pay all costs of the action including a sum representing reasonable attorney's fees for the services rendered by the attorney general's office.

INDIANA

The Indiana statute deliniates those practices which are deemed to be unfair consumer practices. These are:

Sec. 3 (Deceptive Act) (a) The act of a supplier in representing, orally or in writting, as to the subject of a consumer transaction furnished by such supplier, any of the following is a deceptive act:

1. That such subject of a consumer transaction has sponsorship, approval, performance, characteristics, accessories, uses or benefits it does not have which the supplier knows or should reasonably know it does not have;

2. That such subject of a consumer transaction is of a particular standard, quality, grade, style, or model, if it is not, and if the supplier knows or should reasonably know that it is not;

3. That such subject of a consumer transaction is new or unused, if it is not, and if the supplier knows or should reasonably know that it is not;

4. That such subject of a consumer transaction will be supplied to the public in greater quantity than the supplier intends or reasonably expects;

5. That replacement or repair constituting the subject of a consumer transaction is needed, if it is not, and if the supplier knows or should reasonably know that it is not;

6. That a specific price advantage exists as to such subject of a consumer transaction, if it does not, and if the supplier knows or should reasonably know that

11

it does not;

7. That the supplier has a sponsorship, approval or affiliation in such consumer transaction he does not have, and which the supplier knows or should reasonably know that he does not have;

8. That such consumer transaction involves or does not involve a warranty, a disclaimer of warranties or other rights, remedies, or obligations, if the representation is false and if the supplier knows or should reasonably know that the representation is false; or

9. That the consumer will receive a rebate, discount, or other benefit as an inducement for entering into a sale or lease in return for giving the supplier the names of prospective consumers or otherwise helping the supplier to enter into other consumer transactions, if earning the benefit is contingent on a sale or lease occurring after the consumer enters into the original consumer transaction.

A deceptive act may also result from representations within a product or on its packaging. Such false representations constitute a deceptive practice not only on the part of the supplier who places the misrepresentation thereon, but also as to any other supplier who states orally or in writing that the representation is true, so long as the supplier knew or had reason to know that the representations were false.

The supplier is not, however, without a possible defense to the action. If the supplier can show by a preponderance of the evidence that the act resulted from a bona fide error, even though he maintained reasonable procedures to avoid such errors, the act will not be a deceptive one within the meaning of the act. A second defense is also available to the supplier. He may establish that the deceptive act was done in good faith, without his knowledge of its falsity, and in reliance upon the representations of the manufacturer.

Civil lawsuits are authorized under the Indiana statute and may take the form of individual or class actions. In either case the court may award actual damages and reasonable attorney fees incurred in prosecuting the action.

12

The attorney general of Indiana is empowered to seek injunctions against deceptive acts and in general to enforce the various provisions of the Consumer Protection Act. The Consumer Protection Division is a part of the attorney general's office and he is granted authority to investigate claims, mediate claims, and prosecute offenders. The division is also instructed to initiate and maintain an educational program to inform consumers of deceptive sales practices.

IOWA

Like many other states, Iowa has a consumer fraud act which was originally enacted in 1965 and amended in 1970. It is a combination of the advertising and unlawful business practices which many states have adopted as separate statutes.

The act provides that no person shall use any deception, fraud, false pretense, false promise, misrepresentation or concealment, oppression or omission of any material fact so that others rely upon such concealment, suppression or omission in connection with the sale or advertisement of any merchandise, whether or not such person has in fact been mislead, damaged, or deceived thereby. The employment of such practices is an unlawful practice under the act. Likewise, any person who in the advertisement for sale, lease, rent, etc. offers such goods or services at a price which includes a rebate contingent upon the procurement of prospective customers is engaging in an unlawful practice. Any contract which contains such contingent sales price rebate is null and void as to those provisions, but enforceable as to the actual sale, lease, or rental agreement.

There is a specific provision in the act as to the offering of sale or advertising of subdivided lands. Any person who is advertising or selling subdivided lands must first file certain plans, plots, diagrams of water, sewage and electric lines, etc. with the real estate commission of the state. The failure to file or the filing of mistatements constitutes and unlawful practice.

The office of the attorney general in Iowa is empowered to administer and enforce provisions of the consumer protection acts of that state. In so doing, he is conferred the power to subpoena persons, to conduct public hearings, and to provide such forms and promulgate such rules and regulations as may be necessary. Any information which is provided to the attorney general during his investigation or public hearings relating to possible unfair practices under the act cannot be admitted in a criminal prosecution. If there is a subsequent criminal prosecution relating to the subjects testified to or the evidence gathered by the attorney general, the state has the burden of establishing that the information so provided was not used in any manner to further the criminal investigation or prosecution.

The 1970 amendment to the Iowa act takes that provision one step further, and provides that when a civil action is brought the attorney general has the right to require any defendant to give testimony, but no criminal prosecution based upon the transactions about which the defendant is questioned and required to give testimony shall be thereafter brought against such defendant. This, then, amounts to an immunity from criminal prosecution once a civil action is brought and the defendant is required to testify in that civil action or in the investigation of that civil action.

Once the attorney general begins his investigation and employs his subpoena power, a defendant who fails to respond to that subpoena is subject to judicial punishment. A court, based upon the attorney general's allegations of refusal to abide by this subpoena, may grant injunctive relief restraining the sale or advertisement of any merchandise by such persons. Further, the court may dissolve a corporation created under the laws of the state of Iowa or may revoke or suspend the certificate of authority of a foreign corporation doing business in that state or may grant such other relief as required under the circumstances.

The attorney general is authorized to obtain injunctions against persons who are engaging or are about to engage in an unlawful practice as established by the act. The courts further are authorized to return any monies or properties which may have been acquired by means of any practice declared unlawful by the terms of the act. To insure the return of such monies or property the court may appoint a receiver.

A receiver, once appointed, has the power to sue, collect, receive and take into his possession all the goods and chattels, rights and credits, monies and effects, lands and tenements, books, records, documents, papers, chose in an action, bills, notes and property of every description which were obtained by the defendant by any practice declared to be illegal and prohibited by the act. If the property was commingled with the properties rightfully belonging to the defendant, the receiver has the authority to sell and convey the property so as to return the rightful amount to the person who has suffered damages by reason of the unlawful practice.

Since the act contains unfair advertising provisions, the normal exclusions as to owners or publishers of newspapers, magazines or printed matter are provided. Owners and operators of radio or television stations are granted exemptions. These exemptions are, of course, based upon the fact that the owner, publisher or operator has no knowledge of the intent, design or purpose of the advertiser. Advertisements which comply with the rules and regulations of the Federal Trade Commission are, of course, exempt from application of the state act. The state of Iowa Department of Justice, Office of the Attorney General, Consumer Protection Division has published a manual known as "Consumer Protection at the State Level." It is written by Douglas R. Carlson, Assistant Attorney General, Consumer Protection Division. In that manual appears, perhaps, the best explanation of procedures under a consumer fraud act.

The first step under the typical consumer fraud act is the receipt of a complaint either by letter or telephone. The consumer protection division or the attorney general, as the case may be, will usually next contact the company or individual against whom the complaint is filed. The purpose of the initial investigation is to determine whether or not the complaint has any merit. On the one hand, the claim may be warranted but there may be insufficient evidence of fraud to proceed upon the claim. On the other hand, the claim may be groundless.

After the initial investigation has been completed, the further dispostion of the claim depends primarily upon the attitude of the potential violator. Well established, reputable companies will normally adjust the complaint as soon as it is brought to their attention. Thus, there is what may be referred to as a mediation stage. If the complainant and the violator are willing to adjust the matter, then, in most cases, the complaint will not be carried any further. If, however, the complaint cannot be mediated, the result might be a lawsuit brought in the name of the state or a civil lawsuit brought in the name of the individual consumer. Most companies are desirous of protecting their reputations and obviously want to adjust claims before the lawsuit stage.

In those states which employ criminal prosecution as deterrance to unfair practices, the complaint may result in the criminal prosecution and the levying of substantial fines.

This procedure of enforcing the state's statutes can be employed instead of, or contemporaneously with, the bringing of a private lawsuit.

15

The Division of Consumer Protection in the state of Kentucky was created to encompass the following activities:

1. To promote the coordination of consumer protection activities that all departments, divisions, and branches of state, county, and city government are concerned with;

2. To assist, advise, and cooperate with federal, state, and local agencies and officials to protect and promote the interest of the consumer public; to advise the governor and the legislature in all matters concerning consumer affairs;

3. To conduct investigations, research studies, and analysis of matters affecting health, safety, the human environment, the market place, and all other consumer affairs and take appropriate action; to communicate the view of the consumer to state, county, and city agencies and officials;

4. To study the operation of all laws, rules, regulations, orders, and state policies affecting consumers, and recommend to the legislature new legislation, rules, regulations, orders, and policies in the consumers' interests;

5. To organize and hold conferences on problems affecting consumers, to undertake activities to encourage business, industry, and the professions, and others offering goods or services, to maintain high standards of honesty, fair business practices, and public responsibilities in the production, promotion and sale of consumer goods and services;

6. To provide a central clearing house of information for all citizens of the commonwealth by collecting and compiling consumer complaints and inquiries and forwarding them to the proper governmental agencies if appropriate;
     It shall be the further responsibility of the

division to maintain records indicating the final disposition by the agency of any matter so referred;

7. To organize, promote, and conduct consumer education programs within the commonwealth; to cooperate with and establish necessary liason with consumer organizations;

8. A. To appear before any federal, state, or local governmental branch, commission, department, rate-making or regulatory body or agency to represent and be heard on behalf of consumers' interest;

   B. To be made a real party in interest to any action in behalf of consumer interests involving a quasi-judicial or rate-making proceeding of any state or local governmental branch, commission, department, agency, or rate-making body, whenever deemed necessary and advisable in the consumers' interest by the attorney general;

9. To perform such other acts as may be incidental to the exercise of the functions, powers, and duties set forth in the Kentucky revised statutes.

These powers, duties, and functions of the division that have been set forth are representative of the powers, duties, and functions of most of the states' consumer divisions.

The unlawful practices statute of Kentucky makes it unlawful to engage in false, misleading, or deceptive acts or practices while in the conduct of any trade or business. This includes actual fraudulent misrepresentation in the sale of goods or services and in the advertisement of same. The normal exemption for owners or publishers of newspapers, and owners or operators of radio or television stations are provided for in the statute.

The attorney general in the state of Kentucky is empowered to enforce the unfair practices statute and is granted the right to seek injunctive proceedings in the state courts. The attorney general may obtain a restraining order when he establishes, to the satisfaction of the court, that a consumer is about to suffer immediate harm, loss, or injury from the acts or practices of a vendor. The vendor then has the opportunity to seek a dissolution of that restraining order by judicial process.

17

Like courts in other states, the courts in Kentucky are authorized to appoint receivers to assure that consumers will receive their monies or properties payed to a vendor as a result of the unfair practice.

Consumers are authorized to bring civil actions when they have actually suffered damages by reason of the unfair practices committed against them in any transaction which is made for a personal or family reason. The consumer may receive actual monetary damages or, in the proper cases, equitable relief. Further, the consumer may receive punitive damages as a punishment to the vendor for committing such unlawful practices. In addition, a plaintiff in such action is entitled to a reasonable amount as attorney's fees and his costs of suit. Such civil suits must be brought within two years after the actual violation of the Kentucky law, or within one year of the attorney general terminating any action with respect to that transaction, whichever is later.

The attorney general is authorized to accept written assurance of voluntary future compliance by any person, firm, corporation, or business which has committed an unfair practice or is about to commit such unfair practice. This voluntary assurance is not to be considered an admission of violation for any purpose, but simply provides to such business, the opportunity to show its good faith and to adjust the complaint made.

The attorney general of Kentucky has subpoena power and the power to fully investigate any complaint by gathering all documentary evidence needed for that investigation.

In addition to the general unfair practice statute, Kentucky has enacted a referral selling law. That act prohibits the seller or lessor from giving or offering a rebate or discount to the buyer or lessee as an inducement for sale or lease in consideration of the buyer giving to the seller the names of prospective purchasers, or otherwise aiding the seller or lessor in making a sale or lease to another person. Of course, to be an unfair practice the rebate, discount, or other value must be contingent upon an event subsequent to the time the buyer or lessee agrees to buy or lease. If a violation of this provision occurs, the agreement is unenforceable and the buyer or lessee may at his option rescind the agreement or retain the goods delivered and the benefit of any services performed without any obligation to pay for them.

Kentucky also has a typical homes solicitation sales act. Homes solicitation is defined under that act as "a sale of goods

18

or services in which the seller or person acting for him engages in a personal solicitation of the sale at a residence of the buyer and the buyer's agreement or offer to purchase is there given to the seller or a person acting for him." It does not include a sale made persuant to prior negotiations between the parties at a business establishment or a fixed location where goods or services are offered or exhibited for sale.

A home solicitation may be cancelled by the buyer until midnight of the third business day after the day on which the buyer signs an agreement or offer to purchase. Cancellation occurs when notice is given, and the mailing or posting of the cancellation is sufficient. Cancellation need not be in any particular form.

In one instance, however, a buyer may not cancel a solicitation. If the buyer requests the seller to provide the services without delay because of an emergency; and the seller in good faith makes a substantial performance of the contract before the buyer gives notice of cancellation; and the goods cannot be returned in substantially the same condition as received by the buyer; a cancellation will be ineffective.

Although the buyer may cancel the transaction by any written expression of his intention to cancel, the seller is under an obligation to provide the buyer with a written statement. That statement must appear as follows: "If this agreement was solicited in your residence and you do not want the goods or services, you may cancel this agreement by mailing a notice to the seller."

The notice must say that the consumer does not want the goods or services and must be mailed before midnight of the third business day after the agreement is signed. The notice must be mailed to the address of seller given. Failure of the seller to give such notice to the buyer extends the buyer's time in which he may cancel. The buyer may cancel at any time until he has received such notification. Until he does receive such, his cancellation may be in any form whatsoever.

When a cancellation is made, the seller must tender back to the buyer any payments the buyer has made, along with any note or other evidence of indebtedness. If there were goods traded in, they must be tendered back by the seller to the buyer in substantially as good condition as when received. If the seller fails to return goods traded in, the buyer may elect to recover an amount equal to the trade-in allowance stated in the agreement.

The seller is not, however, without any redress for the

cancellation. He may retain as a cancellation fee 5% of the cash price not in excess of the cash down payment. If, however, the seller fails to comply with his obligations under this act he is not entitled to retain his cancellation fee. Until the seller has complied with his obligations, the buyer may retain possession of the goods delivered to him and is granted a statutory lien on the goods in his possession or under his control for any recovery of funds to which he is entitled.

The buyer is also under obligations when he exercises his right to cancel the agreement. He must within a reasonable time after the cancellation, and upon demand by the seller, tender back to the seller any goods delivered by the seller persuant to the sale. His obligation to tender, however, does not require him to move the goods from his residence. If the seller fails to demand possession of the goods within a reasonable time after the cancellation, the goods become the property of the buyer without any obligation on his part to pay for them. A reasonable time is defined in the statute as forty days. The buyer also has the duty to take reasonably good care of the goods in his possession for a reasonable time after cancellation. If the items involved in the sale are services rather than goods, the seller unfortunately is entitled to no compensation except his cancellation fee.

Kentucky has also legislated in the specific area of unsolicited goods. When unsolicited goods are delivered to a person, he has the absolute right to refuse to accept them and is not bound to return the goods. The act specifically provides that these unsolicited goods are deemed to be a gift to the recipient who is free to use them in any manner whatsoever after receipt, without any obligation for the payment thereof. Although the person receiving unsolicited goods is not prevented from returning the goods to the sender, the sender is, of course, taking a chance upon delivering unsolicited goods. Chances are he will receive no payment and not have the goods returned. The term unsolicited is not defined under the statute, but it does not include any merchandise requested by the recipient or merchandise which is addressed to or intended for another person and which the recipiant received by mistake.

An interesting part of the consumer protection package in the state of Kentucky pertains to used automobiles. Under that statute, it is unlawful for any motor vehicle dealer or moter vehicle salesman to refuse to furnish upon request of the prospective purchaser the name of the previous owner of any used car offered for sale. Violation of that statute can result in a fine of not less than fifteen dollars nor more than two hundred dollars, or imprisionment of not more than thirty days, or both. Violations of other provisions of the Kentucky statutes can result in fines up to twenty-five thousand dollars, depending upon the particular violation.

MARYLAND

The Consumer Protection Division in Maryland was created in 1967. That agency reports now handling approximately two thousand requests and inquiries per week, in addition to performing its other functions of mediation, legislation, education, and investigation. Through the efforts of the division, the state legislature has enacted legislation covering a wide range of consumer problems, including unordered merchandise through the mail, a comprehensive system of meat inspection, referral selling, unsolicited credit cards, home solicitation sales (seventy-two-hour right to cancel), odometer setbacks, return of security deposits for tenants, phony games and prizes in promotions, and unit pricing.

Some of Maryland's enactments are of particular interest. The unit pricing law requires sellers to provide shoppers with the total price of goods sold in supermarkets as well as the unit price. This allows a shopper to compare effectively brands and sizes before choosing a product.

It is a criminal offense in Maryland to reset an odometer with the intent to defraud a prospective used car buyer. In the same piece of legislation, an automobile dealer may lose his license when he willfully refuses to honor a new car guarantee or warranty. The recutting or regrooving of tires below original tire standards is also prohibited by the act.

MASSACHUSETTS

Massachusetts has enacted a comprehensive system of consumer protection statutes. These acts cover the following subjects: false advertising; deceptive advertising of guarantees; deceptive pricing; general misrepresentations; referral schemes; advertising or offering to sell on an "easy credit" basis; repairs and services including warranties and service contracts; door-to-door sales and home improvement transactions; private home study, business, technological, social-skills and career schools -- correspondence and other; private

21

employment agencies and business schemes; lay-away plans; pricing and refund; return and cancellation privileges; subscription and mail orders; new-for-used, substitution of products; failure to deliver.

The attorney general of the state is authorized to investigate and prosecute persons or firms who have violated any of the business practices acts. While there is not a particular definition of unfair methods of competition and unfair or deceptive acts or practices in the conduct of trade or business, the act does specify that the courts are to be guided by the interpretations given by the Federal Trade Commission and the Federal Courts to Section 5 (a) (1) of the Federal Trade Commission Act.

The advertising provisions of the statute give the following definitions which are helpful in understanding the type of practices this and other state statutes seek to prevent.

"ADVERTISEMENT," "ADVERTISING," "ADVERTISE"

Any commercial message in any newspaper, magazine, leaflet, flyer, or catalog, on radio, television, public address system, or made in person, in direct mail literature or other printed material, or any interior or exterior sign or display, any window display, in any point of transaction literature or price tag which is delivered or made available to a customer or prospective customer in any manner whatsoever is an advertisement.

"BAIT ADVERTISING"

"Bait advertising" is an alluring but insincere offer to sell a product which the advertiser does not intend or want to sell. Its purpose is to switch consumers from buying the advertised product in order to sell something else, usually at a higher price or on a basis more advantageous to the advertiser. The primary aim of a bait advertisement is to obtain leads as to persons interested in buying a product of the type so advertised.

"BLIND ADVERTISING"

An advertisement which has the tendency to induce consumers to contact the advertiser and which fails to reveal that the primary purpose of the advertisement is the sale of goods or services, and fails to reveal the identity of the advertiser is "blind advertising."

22

The statute prohibits the following advertising tactics:

FALSE ADVERTISING

A. No advertisement containing an offer to sell a product shall be made when the offer is not a bona fide effort to sell the advertised product.

B. No statement or illustration shall be used in any advertisement which creates a false impression of the grade, quality, make, value, currency of model, size, color, usability or origin of the product offered, or which may otherwise misrepresent the product in such a manner that later, on disclosure of the true facts, there is a likelihood that the buyer may be switched from the advertised product to another.

    1. Even though the true facts are subsequently made known to the buyer, the law is violated if the first contact or interview is secured by deception.

C. No act or practice shall be engaged in by an advertiser or seller to discourage the purchase of the advertised product as part of a bait scheme to sell another product.

For example, among acts or practices which will be considered in determining if an advertisement is a bona fide offer are:

    1. The refusal to show, demonstrate, or sell the product offered in accordance with the terms of the offer.

    2. The disparagement by acts or words of the advertised product or disparagement with respect to the guarantee, credit terms, availability of service, repairs or parts, or in any other respect, in connection with it.

    3. The failure to have available at all outlets listed in the advertisement a sufficient quantity of the advertised product to meet reasonably anticipated demands, unless the advertisement clearly and adequately discloses that supply is limited and/or the product is available only at designated outlets.

    4. The refusal to take orders for the advertised product to be delivered within a reasonable period of time.

    5. The showing or demonstrating of a product which is defective, unusable, or impractical for the purpose represented or implied in the advertisement.

    6. Use of a sales plan or method of compensation for salesmen, or penalizing salesmen, designed to prevent or discourage them from selling the advertised product.

D. No practice shall be pursued by an advertiser or seller in the event of sale of the advertised product of obtaining or attempting to obtain a rescission of the sale for the purpose of selling another product in its stead. Among acts or practices which are relevant in determining if the initial sale was in good faith, and not a stratagem to sell another product are:

1. Accepting a deposit for the advertised product, then switching the buyer to a higher-priced product;

2. Failure to make delivery of the advertised product within a reasonable time or make a refund;

3. Disparagement by acts or words of the advertised product, or disparagement with respect to the guarantee, credit terms, availability of service, repairs, or in any other respect, in connection with it;

4. The delivery of the advertised product which is defective, unusable or impractical for the purpose represented or implied in the advertisement. Sales of the advertised product do not preclude the existence of a bait-and-switch scheme if the sales are a mere incidental by-product of the fundamental plan and are intended to provide an aura of legitimacy to the over-all operation.

There are specific regulations pertaining to the advertising of guarantees. Certain disclosures must be made when a guarantee is advertised. The advertisement must contain the nature and extent of the guarantee, including what the product or part thereof is guaranteed, what characteristics or properties of the product are covered, the duration of the guarantee, what the person claiming under the guarantee must do to fulfill his obligations thereunder, and the manner in which the guarantor will perform, as well as his identity.

Special attention is paid to those guarantees which are adjusted on a pro rata basis. Full disclosure of how the adjustment is to be made must be given. The Massachusetts regulations give the following example of such a guarantee and the disclosures that must be given:

Example: During the course of a sale, "A" sells to "B" for $20.00 and with a twelve-month guarantee a battery that he regularly sells for $25.00. After six months the battery proves defective. If "A" adjusts on the basis of the price "B" paid, $20.00, "B" will only have to pay one-half of $20.00, or $10.00, for a new battery. If "A" instead adusts on the basis of the regular selling price, "B" will owe one-half of $25.00, or $12.50, for a new battery. The guarantor would be required to disclose here the following: that this was a twelve-month guarantee; that the regular selling price, rather than the actual sale price, would be used in the adjustment; that there would be an adjustment on the basis of the time that the battery was used; and, that he would not pay the adjustment amount in cash, but would make an adjustment on a new battery, if such be the case.

Other disclosures must be made depending upon the type of guarantee offered.

"Satisfaction or your money back," "ten-day free trial," or similar representations will be construed as a guarantee that the full purchase price will be refunded promptly at the option of the buyer.

If such guarantee is subject to any conditions or limitations whatsoever, they shall be disclosed.

Example: A rose bush is advertised under the representation, "Satisfaction or your money back." The guarantor requires return of the product within a year of purchase date before he will make refund. These limitations, i.e., "return" and "time" shall be clearly and conspicuously disclosed in the ad.

When a product is represented as "guaranteed for life" or as having a "lifetime guarantee," the meaning of the term "life" or "lifetime" should be explained.

A seller or manufacturer shall not advertise or represent that a product is guaranteed when he cannot or does not promptly and scrupulously fulfill his obligations under the guarantee.

The term "unconditionally guaranteed" should not be used when a guarantee is restricted in any manner other than as to time, and, when there is a time limit, it should be clearly disclosed (e.g., "unconditionally guaranteed for three years"). An "unconditional guarantee" is considered as an undertaking on the part of the guarantor either to refund the full purchase price of the product so guaranteed or to repair or replace such product should it prove defective in any respect, all at the option of the buyer.

Massachusetts has a comprehensive enactment on repairs and services including warranties and service contracts. Since many other states do not have specific statutes it is set forth herein.

A. Repairs and Services. It shall be an unfair and deceptive act or practice to:

1. Fail to provide in advance to a customer upon request a written estimate of the cost to the customer of the anticipated repairs, or the basis upon which the charge to the

customer will be made and the reasonably expected time to accomplish such repairs, including any charge for re-assembly of any parts disassembled for inspection or any service charge to be imposed;

1. Make or charge for repairs which have not been authorized by the customer;

3. Fail to disclose, in the case of an in-home service call where the consumer has initially contacted the repair-man, that a service charge will be imposed even though no repairs are effected, before the repairman goes to the con-sumer's home;

4. Represent that repairs are indicated to be necessary when such is not a fact;

5. Represent that repairs have been made when such is not a fact;

6. Represent that the goods being inspected or diagnosed are in a dangerous condition or that the customer's con-tinued used of them may be harmful to him when such is not a fact;

7. Materially understate or mistate the estimated cost of repair services;

8. Fail to provide the customer with an itemized list of repairs performed and the reason for such repairs, including:

    a. A list of parts and statement of whether they are new, used, or rebuilt, and the cost thereof to the customer; and

    b. The number of hours of labor charged and the name of the mechanic performing the service; pro-vided, however, that the requirements of (b) shall be satisfied by the statement of a flat rate price if such repairs are customarily done and billed on a flat rate price basis.

B. Warranties. It shall be an unfair and deceptive act or practice to fail to perform or fulfill any promises or obligations arising under a warranty. The utilization of a deceptive warranty is unlawful.

Language intended to limit or modify the warrantor's obli-gations under a warranty shall not operate to limit the warrantor's liability, notwithstanding the limiting language, if the warrantor fails to perform under the warranty; provided, however, that no language of limitation otherwise unenforceable by statute or regulation shall be enforceable. This regulation in

for which the supplier knows the consumer will be unable to meet payments.

PENNSYLVANIA

In 1968, Pennsylvania created a Bureau of Consumer Protection. Its duties and functions include investigatory powers of commercial and trade practices, fraud, misrepresentation, and deception in the sale, servicing, and financing of consumer goods and products. The primary piece of legislation in Pennsylvania upon which the bureau relies is the Unfair Trade Practices and Consumer Protection Law.

Unfair methods of competition and unfair or deceptive acts or practices are defined in the act. Unfair methods of competition and unfair or deceptive acts or practices mean any one or more of the following:

Passing off goods or services as those of another;

Causing likelihood of confusion or of misunderstanding as to the source, sponsorship, approval, or certification of goods or services;

Causing likelihood of confusion or of misunderstanding as to affiliation, connection, or association with, or certification by, another;

Using deceptive representations or designations of geographic origin in connection with goods or services;

Representing that goods or services have sponsorship, approval, characteristics, ingredients, uses, benefits, or quantities that they do not have, or that a person has a sponsorship, approval, status, affiliation, or connection that he does not have;

Representing that goods are original or new if they are deteriorated, altered, reconditioned, reclaimed, used, or secondhand;

Representing that goods or services are of a particular standard, quality, or grade, or that goods are of a particular style or model if they are of another;

37

no way limits, modifies, or supersedes any other statutory or regulatory provisions dealing with warranties.

C. Service Contracts. It shall be an unfair and deceptive trade practice to fail to disclose in writing, fully and conspicuously, in simple and readily understandable language that a service contract charge will be imposed if the consumer wishes to insure that repairs will be made to a purchased product so that it will operate properly. It shall also be an unfair and deceptive trade practice to fail to disclose in writing, fully, clearly, and conspicuously, in simple and readily understandable language, that a consumer is paying a lower price for goods or services in exchange for a waiver of his warranty rights.

General provisions of the Massachusetts statute regarding private home study, business, technological, social-skills, and career schools are as follows:

A. False Advertising. The making or causing, or permitting to be made or published, any false or deceptive statement or representation, or any statement or representation which has the tendency or capacity to mislead or deceive students, prospective students, or the public, by way of advertising or otherwise concerning private home study, business, technological, career, or social-skills schools, their activities in attempting to enroll students, or concerning the character, nature, quality, value, or scope of any course of instruction or educational service offered, its influence in obtaining employment for its students, or in any other material respect, is an unfair and deceptive trade practice.

B. False Representation as to Earnings. The making of false or deceptive statements or representations or any statement or representation which has the tendency or capacity to mislead or deceive students, prospective students, or the public regarding actual or probable earnings or opportunities in any vocation or field of activity is an unfair and deceptive trade practice.

It is unfair and deceptive practice in the sale or offering for sale of consumer services for a school or person subject to this regulation to represent or imply in advertising or otherwise that persons employed in a particular position earn a stated salary or income or "up to" the stated salary or income unless certain circumstances set forth in the statute exist.

C. Misrepresentation of Opportunity. The making of false, untrue, or deceptive statements or representations, or any statement or representation which has the tendency or capacity to mislead or deceive students, prospective students, or the public regarding any opportunities in any vocation or field of activity as a result of the completion of any given course of instruction or

27

educational service is an unfair and deceptive trade practice.

D. False Representations as to Student Employment or a School's Connection with or Approval by the United States Government or the Commonwealth. The making of false or deceptive statements or representations or any statement or representation which has the tendency or capacity to mislead or deceive students, prospective students, or the public as to services to be rendered in connection with the securing or attempting to secure employment for students, or as to the influence or connection of any school or schools with any branch, department, or establishment of the United States government or with the Commonwealth of Massachusetts is an unfair and deceptive trade practice.

It is an unfair and deceptive practice for a school or a person subject to this regulation to advertise or represent that the school or instruction course has been approved by any government agency without clearly and conspicuously indicating the scope, nature, and terms of that approval, particularly as to how the approval applies to the quality of instruction and the truth of the statements contained in the advertisement or representation. For example, and advertisement or representation shall not state "V.A. Approved," but must state, if such is the case: "V.A. education loans may be used for tuition. V.A. does not review nor guarantee the quality of instruction, nor does it guarantee the truth of the statement in this advertisement."

E. Limited Time Offers. Representing an offer to be limited as to time or otherwise when such is not the fact, with the tendency or capacity to mislead or deceive students, prospective students, or the public is an unfair trade practice.

F. Misrepresenting Offers as "Special." Representing an offer as "special" when it is in fact the school's regular offer is an unfair and deceptive trade practice.

G. Fictitious Prices. Offering courses of instruction at prices purported to be reduced from what are in fact marked up or fictitious prices is an unfair and deceptive trade practice.

H. Money Back Agreements. It is an unfair and deceptive trade practice for any private school subject to these regulations to use, directly or indirectly, any so-called money-back guarantee, refund agreement, or other similar guarantee, agreement, or contract between school and student.

I. Misleading Scholarship Offers. Making offers of scholarships or partial scholarships in such a manner as to mislead or deceive students or prospective students into the belief that such offers are real when in fact they are not is an unfair and

28

deceptive trade practice.

J. Misuse of the Word "Free." Representing any commodity or service as "free" when in fact such commodity or service is regularly included as part of the course of instruction or service is an unfair and deceptive trade practice.

K. Deception in Issuance of Diplomas, Degrees. It is an unfair and deceptive trade practice for any private school subject to these regulations to issue any certificate or diploma or to confer any degree which misrepresents the course of study or instruction covered or completed or the accomplishments or standing of the student receiving such certificate, diploma, or degree.

L. Misrepresenting Faculty. Making a statement or representation through advertising or otherwise that a certain individual or individuals are members of the faculty of the school or are members of its advisory board or authors of its instructional material when they are not, or when they provide no or only token services or advice, or the making of statements or representations as to the value of any former connection with the United States government or the Commonwealth of Massachusetts as an aid to securing employment which are false or misleading is an unfair and deceptive trade practice.

M. Misrepresentation as to Personal Instruction. The representation through advertising or otherwise that students are given personal instruction by the head of the institution or a department head thereof who provides no or only token instruction is an unfair and deceptive trade practice.

N. Deceptive "Help Wanted" Advertising. The use of "help wanted" or other employment columns in a newspaper or other publication to get in touch with prospective students in such a manner as to lead such prospective students into the belief that a job is offered is an unfair and deceptive trade practice.

O. Blind Advertising. The use of "blind" advertisements or sales literature to attract prospective students when such advertisements or literature fail to set forth that courses of instruction or other educational services are being offered is an unfair and deceptive trade practice.

P. Deceptive Language in General. The use of language in any form which has the tendency or capacity to mislead or deceive students, prospective students, or the public is an unfair and deceptive trade practice.

Q. Unqualified Students. Inducing the enrollment or retention of a student for any course of instruction or training for a job

or position for which the school knows or has reason to know the student is unfit by reason of educational or permanent physical disqualification or other material disqualification is an unfair and deceptive trade practice.

Massachusetts has also seen fit to protect consumers from unduly harsh collection techniques. While federal legislation prohibits what amounts to extortionate credit collection techniques, very few states have gone as far as Massachusetts in limiting extra-judicial collection policies.

That act provides: "No one who is a creditor, or an assignee of a creditor, of a natural person present or residing in Massachusetts who has incurred a debt primarily for personal, family, or household purposes shall collect or attempt to collect such debt in an unfair, deceptive, or unreasonable manner."

Under the statute, it is illegal for creditors to use unfair or deceptive practices to collect money owed to them by debtors.

A creditor may not tell or threaten to tell the debtor's relatives, employer, or other close associates about the debt in an attempt to encourage payment. However, a creditor may notify a credit bureau about the debt. But he must tell the creditor he is going to do so. Creditors also must notify debtors if they intend to hire an agent or attorney to collect the debt.

It is illegal for creditors to send debtors collection notices in envelopes that indicate or imply that a debt is owed.

It is illegal for a creditor to contact a debtor directly if the debtor has asked the creditor to deal with his attorney.

The creditor may not send the debtor forged or "legal-looking" documents to imply that court or legal action has been taken against the debtor.

It is illegal for a creditor to contact the debtor in a way that might harrass or embarrass the debtor.

The creditor MAY NOT telephone the debtor at unreasonable hours, telephone the debtor repeatedly and frequently, threaten to use violence if the debtor does not pay, use offensive language in talking to the debtor, nor threaten to take any action against the debtor that is not usually taken in his type of business.

MISSOURI

The state of Missouri has enacted legislation which it entitles "Merchandising Practices." This piece of legislation generally follows the pattern of other state legislation dealing with unfair practices to the consumer. The term merchandise as used

in the caption of the statute and within its various provisions includes any objects, wares, goods, commodities, intangibles, real estate, or services.

Under the terms of the act it is unlawful to use or employ any deception, fraud, false pretense, false promise, misrepresentation or concealment, suppression or omission, in connection with the sale or advertisement of any merchandise.

The administration of the statutory provisions are vested in the attorney general of the state who may investigate and prosecute alleged violators of the statute. Injunctions may be obtained and any person who violates the terms of an injunction faces a penalty of up to five thousand dollars for each violation. Prosecution by the attorney general does not prohibit any civil action by an individual consumer.

The Missouri statute also encompasses a section on unsolicited merchandise. When unsolicited merchandise is delivered to a consumer he may either refuse to accept delivery of it or, if he wishes, he may treat the merchandise as a gift and thereafter use or dispose of it in any way he wishes. In so doing, he incurs no obligation to the seller.

NEW HAMPSHIRE

In 1970, New Hampshire enacted a statute designated as "Regulation of Business Practices for Consumer Protection." This particular act combines general unlawful or deceptive trade practices with false and misleading advertising. It generally contains the standard provisions describing the acts which shall constitute deceptive or unlawful trade practices. These include the procedures of vendors which would, in all likelihood, cause confusion or misunderstanding among consumers as to the characteristics, ingredients, benefits, or quantities of merchandise; and also confusion as to the identity of the goods, their sponsorship, approval, or certification. Likewise, the disparaging of the goods and services of another by false or misleading representations constitutes a deceptive practice under the New Hampshire statute. One who advertises the sale of goods or services, but does not intend to supply reasonably expectable public demand, or who makes false or misleading statements of fact concerning the reasons for existence of or amounts of price reductions is in violation of the act.

One who claims an exemption under the act has the burden of establishing that exemption. Publishers, broadcasters, and the

like, who disseminate information without knowledge of its deceptive character, are exempt from the act as are transactions which are covered by Federal Trade Commission regulations. The attorney general is vested with authority to enforce the provisions of the act, and may establish such rules and regulations as are necessary or desirable for the proper administration of the act. The attorney general may seek temporary or permanent restraining orders against those persons who violate or are likely to violate provisions of the act. Prior to taking any specific action, the attorney general must give the alleged violator ten days notice, thus providing him with the opportunity to amicably adjust the situation. Violation of the deceptive trade practices act is a misdemeanor and a violater thereof may be fined up to one thousand dollars. If an injunction is issued and then violated, the fine can be as high as ten thousand dollars for each violation.

As in all consumer protection statutes, the person or division authorized to enforce the statute is granted investigatory rights including the power to subpoena books, records, and the like, along with examining persons who can shed some light upon the alleged violation. Failure to abide by requests of the attorney general in securing this information can result in fines up to five thousand dollars. If it is found that a particular violator, American or foreign, is one who habitually violates the injunctions granted under the auspices of the statute, the attorney general may petition the court for dissolution, suspension, or forfeiture of that corporation's right to do business in the state.

A civil suit for restitution of all goods or services lost by the consumer is authorized by the statute and the court in hearing such a case may award, along with restitution of goods or monies, all legal costs and expenses incurred by the plaintiff in the prosecution of the lawsuit. It is interesting to note that the act specifically provides that in those cases where the cause of action is based upon confusion of identity of goods and/or manufacturer, sponsor, or the like, the plaintiff is required to prove only that such confusion or misunderstanding is likely and not that it actually transpired.

NEW MEXICO

New Mexico has divided its consumer legislation into three basic areas: unfair trade practices, false advertising, and the land subdivision act.

An unfair or deceptive trade practice is defined in the

statute as: "any false or misleading oral or written statement, visual description or other representation of any kind, knowingly made in connection with the sale, lease, rental, or loan of goods or services, in the extension of credit for a collection of debts by any person in the regular course of trade or commerce which may tend to or does deceive or mislead any person, and includes: . . ." The inclusions under that definition are the standard deceptive trade practices: confusion of the identity of goods; confusion as to the affiliation; representing used goods to be new; falsely misrepresenting the quality or grade of the goods; disparaging the goods and services of another by false or misleading representations; failure to intend to supply a reasonable demand for the goods; and the like.

Unique in the New Mexico statute is a provision that packaging goods for sale without authorization in a container that bears a trademark or trade name identified with goods formerly packaged in the container is an unfair trade practice. This, of course, would be a violation of federal statutes on trademark regulation.

The act distinguishes between a "deceptive trade practice" and an "unconcionable trade practice." The latter means any act or practice in the sale, lease, rental, or loan, or in connection with the offering for sale, lease, rental, or loan, of any goods or services, or in the extension of credit, or in the collection of debts, which to a person's detriment: (1) takes advantage of the lack of knowledge, ability, experience, or capacity of a person to a grossly unfair degree; or (2) results in a gross disparity between the value received by the person and the price paid.

The civil fine for violating either the deceptive trade practices act or the unconscionable trade practice act may be as high as five thousand dollars per violation.

The act also covers chain referral sales and strictly prohibits the use of that technique whereby the buyer is induced to purchase merchandise or services upon the promise that he provide the seller with prospective buyers. In return, he will receive a reduction of the price of the goods he purchased by means of a cash rebate, commission, or credit toward the balance due.

It is also a specific violation of the act to willfully misrepresent the age or condition of any motor vehicle. Such misrepresentations include, but are not limited to, resetting the odometer, regrooving the tires, or chassis repair without previously informing the purchaser of the vehicle that such repairs were done. Anyone who violates that section of the act is deemed guilty

of a misdemeanor. The seller of any motor vehicle must, at the time of the sale, provide the following information to the buyer: a description of the vehicle; a statement that to the best of the seller's knowledge there has been no alteration or chassis repair due to a previous wreck; a statement as to the mileage on the vehicle at the time of the sale; a statement that to the best of the seller's knowledge the odometer has not been altered.

As under other statutes, the attorney general is granted authority to seek restraining orders, make settlements of alleged violations and investigate all claims through the use of subpoena power and the like. The act specifically provides for private remedies and in certain incidents the court may award attorney's fees to the prevailing party.

The false advertising act in New Mexico is substantially the same as in other states. It prohibits false advertising which in any way is misleading. This includes not only representations made by statements, but also failure to reveal facts in the advertisement.

Like other states in which sale of land for development purposes is a booming business, the state of New Mexico has enacted a land subdivision act to control such business and to prevent frauds upon consumers. Basically the statute is one of disclosure, and the seller of subdivided land must make written disclosure to the purchaser of the following items:

1. All restrictions or reservations of record which subject the subdivided land to any unusual conditions affecting its use or occupancy;

2. The fact that any street or road facilities have not been accepted for maintenance by governmental agencies when such is the case;

3. Availability of all public utilities in a subdivision, including water, electricity, gas, and telephone facilities;

4. If water is available only from subterranean sources, the average depth of such water within the subdivision;

5. Complete price in financing terms or rental;

6. The existence of blanket encumbances, if there are any, on such subdivision unless such blanketing encumbances provide for a proper release or subordination to such lot or a parcel.

Advertising standards are also provided in the act and willful violation of the advertising standards resulting in misrepresentations can be punished by conviction of a felony, including imprisonment for not more than five years or by a fine of not more than $100,000 or both.

OHIO

Ohio has created a Department of Commerce Consumer Protection Division whose stated purposes are to:

Educate and inform the public in order to make more sophisticated consumers;

Process and resolve complaints and inquiries regarding consumer transactions; and

Do in-depth analysis of specific industries which may need more regulation.

The program of consumer protection is administered through the state attorney general's office and the teeth of the program are the consumer protection statutes enacted in 1972. Home solicitation sales have been examined previously and the Ohio act is in general comparable to other states' legislation which has been analyzed in detail. The cooling-off period is provided for all sales of thirty-five dollars or more consummated in the consumer's home.

The Consumer Sales Practices Act permits the attorney general to bring an action to obtain a declaratory judgment that an act or practice violates the provisions of the act. Restraining orders may be obtained against violators, and a supplier who violates such an order is subject to a penalty of up to five thousand dollars for each day of violation.

Class actions may be brought on behalf of consumers who have been damaged by acts of suppliers in violation of the statute, and consumers may recover, depending upon the type of suit brought, actual damages, property or funds paid, rescission of

the transaction, injunction, or other appropriate relief.

Although the Ohio statute speaks of "suppliers" as those persons subject to the provisions of the act, that term includes sellers, lessors, assignors, franchisors, and any other person engaged in the business of affecting or soliciting consumer transactions, whether or not he deals directly with the consumer.

Deceptive acts and practices as well as unconscionable acts or practices are unlawful whether they occur before, during, or after the actual transaction. A clear, concise explanation of the types of practices prohibited was published by the Department in a fact sheet, available for public reading.

Deceptive transactions include charging an extra fee (above the estimated repair price) to take an appliance out of the home for repair unless the consumer is informed of this extra charge before the appliance is removed to the repair shop; advertising an item on sale but failing to have an adequate supply of items to meet the demand; using "bait and switch" techniques in a sales transaction; misrepresenting an item pictorially in an advertisement; delivering a product that is defective and then refusing to correct the defect or adjust the price; failing to make delivery of a purchased item within a reasonable length of time; making claims about a product which are untrue -- for example, to claim an automobile has had only one owner when it has had many. It is also deceptive to turn back the odometer on a car.

Unconscionable acts or practices are differentiated from deceptive practices by the additional feature of knowledge on the part of the supplier or a particular consumer's inability to protect himself because of physical or mental infirmities, ignorance, illiteracy, or inability to understand the language of the agreement. The fact sheet published by the division gives these examples of unconscionable acts or practices:

Charging an exorbitant price for services or merchandise available at a much lower price;

Persuading consumers to enter into transactions from which the consumer receives no substantial benefit;

Making misleading statements which are likely to be of detriment to the consumer;

Encouraging the consumer to enter into a contract

Disparaging the goods, services, or business of another by false or misleading representation of fact;

Advertising goods or services with intent not to sell them as advertised;

Advertising goods or services with intent not to supply reasonably expectable public demand, unless the advertisement discloses a limitation of quantity;

Making false or misleading statements of fact concerning the reasons for, existence of, or amounts of price reductions;

Promising or offering to pay, credit, or allow to any buyer any compensation or regard for the procurement of a contract of purchase with others.

Home solicitation sales of twenty-five dollars or more may be cancelled in Pennsylvania by written notice within two full business days following the sale. The consumer must return the goods purchased and in return the seller must return all payments or other considerations given for the sale.

Civil penalties for violation of an injunctive order may result in a fine of up to five thousand dollars for each violation, and, in addition, the attorney general may seek the dissolution, suspension, or forfeiture of the corporate franchise of any corporation found to have violated the terms of an injunction.

RHODE ISLAND

Rhode Island, like several other states, has enacted a Home Solicitation Sales Act. Under that particular statute, both the seller and buyer have certain obligations. These are as follows:

Seller's obligations on cancellation.

(a) Except as provided in this section, within twenty (20) days after a solicitation sale has been cancelled the seller shall tender to the buyer any payments made by the buyer and any note or other evidence of indebtedness.

(b) If the down payment includes goods trades in, the goods shall be tendered in substantially as good condition

38

as when received. If the seller fails to tender the goods as provided by this section, the buyer may elect to recover an amount equal to the trade-in-allowance stated in the agreement.

(c) The seller may retain as a cancellation fee five per cent (5%) of the cash price, five dollars ($5.00) or the amount of the cash down payment, whichever is least. If the seller fails to comply with an obligation imposed by this section, or if the buyer avoids the sale on any grounds independent of his right to cancel under this chapter, the seller is not entitled to retain a cancellation fee.

(d) Until the seller has complied with the obligations imposed by this section, the buyer may retain possession of goods delivered to him by the seller and has a lien on the goods for any recovery to which he is entitled.

Buyer's obligations on cancellation.
(a) Except as otherwise provided, within twenty (20) days after a home solicitation sale has been cancelled, the buyer, upon demand, shall tender to the seller any goods delivered by the seller pursuant to the sale, but he is not obligated to tender at any place other than his own address. If the seller fails without interference from the buyer to take possession of such goods within twenty (20) days after cancellation the goods shall become the property of the buyer without obligation to pay for them.

(b) The buyer shall take reasonable care of the goods in his possession both prior to cancellation and during the twenty (20) day period following. During the twenty (20) day period after cancellation, except for the buyer's duty of care, the goods are at the seller's risk.

(c) If the seller has performed any services pursuant to a home solicitation sale prior to its cancellation, the seller is entitled to no compensation except the cancellation fee provided in this chapter. If the seller's services result in the alteration of property of the buyer, the seller shall restore the property to substantially as good condition as it was in at the time the services were rendered.

If a buyer is to cancel the transaction, he must do so not later than midnight three (3) days following his signing the agreement, excluding Sunday and any holiday on which regular mail deliveries are not made. The notice must be sent by registered or certified mail.

A home solicitation sale can only be effective to bind a consumer if the seller provides him with notice of the consumer's right to cancel. The statute sets forth the precise written notice which must be given to the consumer.

Notice to Buyer: (1) Do not sign this agreement if any of the spaces intended for the agreed terms to the extent of then available information are left blank. (2) You are entitled to a copy of this agreement at the time you sign it. (3) You may at any time pay off the full unpaid balance due under this agreement, and in so doing you may be entitled to receive a partial rebate of the finance and insurance charges. (4) The seller has no right to enter unlawfully your premises or commit any breach of the peace to repossess goods purchased under this agreement. (5) You may cancel this agreement if it has not been signed at the main office or a branch office of the seller, provided you notify the seller at his main office or branch office shown in the agreement by registered or certified mail, which shall be posted not later than midnight of the third calendar day after the day on which the buyer signs the agreement, excluding Sunday and any holiday on which regular mail deliveries are not made.

In addition to the home solicitation act, Rhode Island has also enacted a Deceptive Trade Practices Act, and it generally follows the pattern of other state statutes which we have already examined. That statute does, however, provide for private and class actions and those provisions, as illustrative of other states so providing are set forth herein.

Private and class actions.

(a) Any person who purchases or leases goods or services primarily for personal, family, or household

40

purposes and thereby suffers any ascertainable loss of money or property, real or personal, as a result of the use or employment by another person of a method, act, or practice declared unlawful by this act may bring an action under rules of civil procedure in the superior court of the county in which the seller or lessor resides, is found, has his principal place of business, or is doing business, or in the superior court of such county as is otherwise provided by law, to recover actual damages or two hundred dollars ($200), whichever is greater. The court may, in its discretion, award punitive damages and may provide such equitable relief as it deems necessary or proper.

(b) Persons entitled to bring an action under subsection (a) of this section may, if the unlawful method, act, or practice has caused similar injury to numerous other persons similarly situated and if they adequately represent such similarly situated persons, bring an action on behalf of themselves and other similarly injured and situated persons to recover damages as provided for in subsection (a) of this section. In any action brought under this section, the court may in its discretion order, in addition to damages, injunctive or other equitable relief.

(c) Upon commencement of any action brought under subsection (a) of this section the clerk of court shall mail a copy of the complaint or other initial pleading to the attorney general and, upon entry of any judgment or decree in the action, shall mail a copy of such judgment or decree to the attorney general.

(d) In any action brought by a person under this section, the court may award in addition to the relief provided in this section, reasonable attorney's fees and costs.

(e) Any permanent injunction, judgment, or order of the court shall be prima facie evidence in an action brought under this act that the respondent used or employed a method, act, or practice declared unlawful by this act.

As we have seen, some states have seen fit to enumerate specifically the practices which are deemed to be unfair while others simply leave that determination to judicial or administrative interpretation. Texas has enumerated unfair practices in its statute. These practices are:

Passing off goods or services as those of another;

Causing confusion or misunderstanding as to the source, sponsorship, approval, or certification of goods or services;

Causing confusion or misunderstandings as to affiliation, connection, or association with, or certification by another;

Using deceptive representations or designations of geographic origin in connection with goods or services;

Representing that goods or services have sponsorship, approval, characteristics, ingredients, uses, benefits, or quantities that they do not have or that a person has a sponsorship, approval, status, affiliation, or connection that he does not have;

Representing that goods are original or new if they are deteriorated, altered, reconditioned, reclaimed, used, or second hand;

Representing that goods or services are of a particular standard, quality, or grade, or that goods are of a particular style or model, if they are of another;

Disparaging the goods, services, or business of another by false or misleading representations of fact;

Advertising goods or services with intent not to sell them as advertised;

Advertising goods or services with intent not to supply reasonably expectable public demand, unless the advertisement discloses a limitation of quantity;

Making false or misleading statements of fact concerning the reasons for, existence of, or amounts of price reductions;

Engaging in any act or practice which is deceptive to the consumer;

Advertising of a liquidation sale, auction sale, or other sale fraudulently representing that the person is going out of business;

Conduction or sponsoring in connection with the sale of, or offer to sell, goods, merchandise, or anything of value, any contest, sweepstakes, puzzle, or game of chance by which a person may, as determined by drawing, guessing, matching, or chance, receive gifts, prizes, discounts, coupons, certificates, or gratuities if such contest, sweepstakes, puzzle, or game, or the promotion of such contest, sweepstakes, puzzle, or game:

Misrepresents by any means or in any form the participant's chances of winning any such gifts, prizes, discounts, coupons, certificates, or gratuities; or

Fails to disclose to participants in such contest, sweepstakes, puzzle, or game on a permanent poster in case such contest or game is conducted by a retail outlet, or, in case such contest or game is not conducted in a retail outlet, on any card game piece, entry blank, or any paraphernalia required for participation in such contest or game the following:

The geographical area or number of outlets in which the contest or game is proposed to be conducted; an accurate description of each type of gift, prize, discount, coupon, certificate, or gratuities to be made available;

The minimum number of and minimum amount of cash gifts, prizes, discounts, and gratuities to be made available and the minimum number of each other type of gift, prize, discount, coupon, certificate, or gratuity to be made available.

The Texas act contains the normal exemptions for transactions covered by federal agencies, the owners and operators of advertising media, and publishers. Transactions in the insurance business which are covered by other legislation are also exempt. Restraining orders are authorized under the act when it appears that a vendor has engaged in or is about to engage in an unlawful act. The consumer credit commissioner, through the Division of Consumer Protection, is vested with the authority to conduct investigations, require the filing of reports, examine alleged violators, examine the merchandise or samples thereof, and generally do anything necessary and proper to conduct a thorough investigation of any alleged violation of the consumer protection act.

Attempts to thwart the commissioner in his investigation procedure may result in a jail sentence or a fine of not more than five thousand dollars or both. Other penalties under the act may result in fines up to ten thousand dollars.

VERMONT

Vermont has enacted a consumer fraud statute which is enforced by the consumer protection bureau of the state attorney general's office. That legislation is to complement the operation of federal statutes and decisions governing methods of unfair competition and practices. The over-all purpose, is, of course, to protect the public and to encourage fair and honest competition. The act was first put into effect in 1967. The act, beyond specifying unlawful practices, encourages activities to educate consumers in the ways of the market place and to generally promote consumer welfare.

The advertising provisions of the Vermont laws do not apply to owners and publishers of newspapers and magazines and further exempt owners of television and radio stations. These exemptions are included for the obvious reason that such persons cannot absolutely control or, in many cases, be aware of the nature of the advertisements appearing in their publications or on their airways. However, the exemptions to such owners, publishers, or operators are not absolute. They must not have knowledge of the fraudulent intent of the advertiser.

This particular statute allows the attorney general to initiate rules and regulations pertaining to unfair methods of competition and deceptive trade practices. The act provides a right of rescission where the consumer has not received a substantial portion of the goods or services he contracted for, so long as he exercises that right of rescission by delivering or mailing the notice of rescission to the seller's principal place of business on the business day following the day of the transaction. When a rescission is so made, the seller must return to the consumer any monies paid for the goods or services and any and all documents evidencing the consumer's indebtedness to the seller which documents were executed as part of the transaction being rescinded.

The rescission provisions apply to all types of goods and services including, but not limited to, automobiles, mobile homes (when used for personal use), family or household chattels, and also goods used in the area of home improvements, and construction of real property whether or not these are to become fixtures.

Services are likewise included in the rescission provisions, including all types of labor and other services to be used for personal, family, or household reasons.

An important provision of the Vermont statute is the elimination of the holder-in-due-course concept. The holder of a promissory note or other instrument of indebtedness of the consumer takes that note or instrument subject to all the defenses, real or personal, that the consumer would have against the seller in an action on a simple contract, so long as the note or other instrument of indebtedness has been delivered in connection with the contract of purchase signed by the consumer.

An agreement or a cognovit provision of a note is void and of no force and effect against any party. Likewise an assignment of wages is void.

The act specifically sets forth certain practices which if found to exist are taken to be evidence of fraud. Included in such group of prima facie fraudulent acts are the failure to accept the terms and conditions as advertised. These activities create a rebuttable presumption of intent on the part of the seller to defraud the consumer.

Like most of the other state statutes, the Vermont statute authorizes the attorney general to investigate a complaint and bring an action in the name of the state seeking a temporary or permanent injunction. The state courts are authorized to issue such injunctions and are authorized to revoke a certificate of authority of a corporation which has been found to have violated the deceptive trade practices act. The attorney general may obtain an assurance of discontinuance, that is, a written statement of the seller that he will not, in the future, violate the provisions of the act.

The attorney general in making investigations has the power

to subpoena relevant books, records, and memoranda of the sale which shed some light on the alleged violation.

Once a seller has been notified of the alleged violation and attempts to conceal, hide, or destroy any documentation pertaining to the sale, he is subject to a fine of five thousand dollars. The failure to comply with the request of the attorney general for the production of relevant documents can result in the seller being found in contempt of court. Once an injunction has been granted, the failure to abide by such injunction may result in a penalty of not more than ten thousand dollars for each violation.

Civil actions brought by aggrieved consumers are not prohibited by the act. The act provides that the consumer may recover the consideration he has paid, plus a penalty of not more than one thousand dollars.

Vermont, like many other states, has specific enactments enumerating specific unfair trade practices. One such act pertains to chain distributor schemes. Under that act it is an unfair trade practice to promote chain distributorships with solicitations of investments from the public. It is an unfair practice when the scheme serves to promote an imprudent and uneconomical investment. The reason for such legislation is that many individuals do not possess commercial expertise, and are lured by the attractiveness of unrealistic profits without considering actual market conditions and the saleability of their goods or services.

A chain distributorship scheme is a sales device whereby a person, upon a condition that he makes an investment, obtains the right to solicit, or recruit for profit or economic gain additional persons who are granted licenses or rights to perpetuate the chain. The fact that the number of persons who participate is limited or the eligibility for participants is conditioned does not change the identity of the scheme as a chain distribution scheme. It is a violation of the act to promote, offer, or encourage participation in a chain distributor scheme.

Vermont also has a seller's warranty obligation statute. It is a specific violation of that act when a seller gives warranties and then fails to honor them. Express or oral warranties made to induce the consumer to purchase the goods or services must be honored. This does not mean, however, that there may not be situations where the seller would not have to honor warranties. There may be extraordinary circumstances or facts which would make the honoring of the warranty unequitable under the situation.

In Wisconsin, the Department of Agriculture is the controlling body behind the consumer protection efforts of that state.

State legislation generally prohibits unfair methods of competition and unfair trade practices. Guidelines of what unfair competition and unfair trade practices consist of are to be determined by the department through public hearings. The administrative body is then authorized to issue orders enjoining unfair practices and unfair competition.

Like other state statutes, the Wisconsin statute authorizes the bringing of civil suits and the awarding of double damages, costs of suit, and attorney fees.

Willful violations of the unfair competition or trade practices provisions of the statutes or administrative rulings may result in fines from twenty-five hundred to five thousand dollars. Suits may be brought in the name of the state and civil penalties varying from one hundred to ten thousand dollars may result, especially where there has been a violation of an injunction.

An administrative regulation makes it an unfair practice to require a buyer to sign a judgment note for the contract price of certain home remodeling when that note is signed contemporaneously with the contract of purchase. In such a case the department has ruled the contract to be void as a matter of law.

Wisconsin has a separate fraudulent advertising law. Deceptive advertising practices are enumerated and in substance are as follows:

> To fail to state the price of goods and/or services or any other conditions imposed upon receipt of the property or services advertised;

> To advertise sales of items so as to lead the buyer to believe that the goods are offered by a private individual rather than a business firm;

> To advertise for donations by any means or sell merchandise when a part of the price to be donated to an organization, unless the following disclosures are made:
> the minimum amount to be donated stated in dollars; the minimum percentage of the net income to be donated; the minimum percentage of the gross income to be donated.

Other filing requirements are specified in the donation sale situation.

The advertising act requires the posting of certain information by any person, firm, corporation, etc. engaged in the businesses of furs, wearing apparel, furniture, pianos, phonographs, other musical instruments, motor vehicles, stocks, or generally any form of property, real or personal, or the furnishings of any kind of service or investment. These persons must post a sign in a conspicuous place outside the place of business and in any salesroom. The name of the association of business and the actual owner must be disclosed.

The advertising of the sale of motor fuel is specifically regulated by Wisconsin statute, and over-all exemptions are provided to the owners, operators, and publishers of newspapers, magazines, and television and radio stations.

Under the statute it is a deceptive practice to misrepresent the nature of any business. One may not use the terms manufacturer, factory, mill, importer, etc., unless the business is in fact of that nature. Further, it is a deceptive practice to misrepresent the nature of prices being offered. One may not advertise that the prices are wholesale or manufacturer's prices unless the prices truly are.

The Department of Agriculture is authorized to enforce and prosecute violations of the various statutes concerning unfair business practices. Civil actions may still, however, be brought by private consumers. These actions may result in double damages, costs of suit, and attorney fees. There is a three-year statute of limitations in the bringing of such suits.

Since the Department of Agriculture must enforce the various state statutes, it has been given investigatory powers, including the right to subpoena relevant documents, and the power to obtain written statements of future compliance from those who have previously violated the acts.

Violation of the deceptive advertising provisions can bring criminal penalties of up to two hundred dollars, six months in jail, or both. Violation of injunctive orders carry fines from one hundred to ten thousand dollars.

Home solicitation sales is another area of specific legislation in Wisconsin. A home solicitation sale is defined as the selling, leasing, or offering of sale where the sale, lease, or offer is personally solicited or consummated at the residence, place of business, or employment of the buyer or at a seller's transient quarters. Transient quarters include hotel and motel rooms as well as other temporary locations.

Personal solicitation includes telephone calls, person-to-person confrontations, and mailings other than the general advertising catalogues or requests to buy at a regular business location.

Home solicitations have traditionally resulted in representations to the buyer of a unique nature. Basically, the buyer is told that he has been specially selected for an introductory offer or that the seller really doesn't want to sell anything but rather is conducting a survey, or running a test of his product. The warranties made and the sales pitches are imaginative and effective. Recognizing these sales tactics, the Wisconsin legislature has made the following misrepresentations in home solicitations sales unlawful:

> "This is a special offer only being made to a few selected people."

> "We are conducting a survey, test, or research project." (When the real objective is a sale.)

> "This is a special sales promotion offered for a limited time to a limited number of people."

> "We are giving a gift or offering a second product at a nominal charge if you buy our product at the normal price." (This may be a legal procedure if the gift or special offer is not contingent on buying the first product. The second product may be discounted, but the consumer must be made aware of the unit price of each product.)

> "We are offering this product at a special reduced price." (Again, this may be a legal sales promotion so long as there have been substantial sales of the product at the higher price.)

> "We will provide service for a longer period of time than we are obligated to under the terms of our written contract."

> "We will reduce the price of this product if you will allow us to use your name or written statement as an

49

endorsement for our product or service."

It is also a violation of the home solicitation act if misrepresentations are made as to the identity of the seller, the amount of available savings, the length of the sales presentation, the delivery or performance date, the nature of the documents to be executed, and the guarantees or warranties extended.

Interestingly, it is a violation of the act if the seller does not promptly leave the buyer's premises when requested to do so.

OTHER WISCONSIN STATUTES

Among the other areas of specific legislation in Wisconsin is regulation of trade practices in the sale or offering for sale of any wholesale cut or food service plan. Likewise, practices in the building and home improvement business are regulated. Unfair trade practices in that area include model home lure, misrepresentation of the product, bait selling, misrepresentation of the capabilities of the product, the identity of the seller, price and financing, guarantees, date of completion, and maintenance requirements. Competitors may not be disparaged unfairly, and certain disclosures must be made in the contract of sale such as insurance, maintenance, description of product, terms and conditions of financing, warranties and guarantees.

The holder-in-due-course concept is eliminated in home improvement contracts. Every assignee of a home improvement contract takes that contract subject to all claims and defenses of the buyer or his successors in interest arising out of the contract. Thus, an assigne is subject to claims arising out of defects in the material or workmanship which would not affect him if he were a holder in due course under the traditional concept thereof.

A promissory note may not be used in a home improvement transaction unless the following language appears: "This is a home improvement instrument and is non-negotiable."

Thus, every holder of the note takes subject to all other claims and defenses of the maker or obligator.

Wisconsin has also legislated in the areas of mobile home parks, chain distributor schemes, referral selling plans, and deceptive offers of employment.

Deceptive offers of employment usually include those in which the employee is required to make a monetary investment to obtain the employment. If such is the case, any ad promoting the employment must reveal that an investment is necessary. False advertising as to the nature of the employment, amount of earnings, commissions, or other compensation to be earned is prohibited.

Like most other states that have regulated the referral selling plans, Wisconsin prohibits sellers or lessors from giving compensation under such plans, unless the compensation is given or paid prior to the sale.

OTHER STATES

Examination of the states detailed herein gives one a good idea of the type of state legislation that now exists for the consumer's protection. It cannot be urged too strongly that a consumer's particular state statutes should be examined as there are, for all the similarities, many important differences. Most importantly is the type of available remedy. Most states provide only for actions brought in the name of the state by the attorney general while a few have expanded the traditional common law in the area to include class actions under the state statute. This is of extreme importance in that a specific act by a seller may not be violative of common law principles governing consumer transactions but indeed violative of the state statute.

In addition to the states already examined, New York, South Dakota, North Carolina, Washington, and Michigan have provided this writer with materials explaining their consumer protection activities.

Michigan's activities in the consumer legislation area include the regulation of lots, parcels, units, or interests in bonds within real estate subdivisions; the regulation of advertising; regulation of the rate of interest that can be charged; regulation of home solicitation sales; regulation of home improvement installment contracts; regulation of retail installment sales; and many other areas of inspection and regulation.

North Carolina has taken particular interest in land development promotions, especially in the area of vacation and retirement land. The state has an unfair and deceptive trade practices act with a very clear and consice statement of objectives which, in reality, states the objectives of all such statutes.

> The purpose of this section is to declare, and to provide civil legal means to maintain, ethical standards of dealings between persons engaged in business, and between persons engaged in business and

51

the consuming public within this State, to the end
that good faith and fair dealings between buyers and
sellers at all levels of commerce be had in
this State.

In addition to the General Deceptive Trade Practices Act,
South Dakota has legislated in the areas of unsolicitated merchandise, direct solicitation, credit contracts, advertising, and
multilevel distribution plans. The latter refers to referral selling
programs or chain sales.

Endless chain sales are absolutely prohibited and are defined as:

> Any scheme or plan for the disposal or distribution
> of property or services whereby a participant pays a
> valuable consideration for the chance to receive com-
> pensation for introducing one or more additional per-
> sons into participation in the scheme or plan or for the
> chance to receive compensation when the person intro-
> duced by the participant introduces a new participant.

Washington has instructed, by publication, its consuming
public that there are a great variety of public and private agencies
which can be of assistance in solving consumer problems. These
agencies include professional associations, state departments,
better business bureaus, federal agencies, and associations of
manufacturers and retailers.

While federal agencies and state agencies have been examined in some detail, better business bureaus have not been.
Washington reports that there are approximately 140 such bureaus
located in major market centers throughout the United States,
Canada, and other countries. These bureaus have three basic
goals:

> 1. To help maintain a free enterprise market environ-
>   ment in which business can operate profitably, by
>   persuading the business community to control mis-
>   representation and deception in advertising and
>   selling;
>
> 2. To help maintain a consumer climate favorable to
>   industrial and commercial growth and vitality, by
>   demonstrating to the public the willingness and
>   ability of the business community, to remove the

causes of justifiable criticism of advertising and selling;

3. To help safeguard a community's buying power, by directing it into legitimate channels of business through various public information and education services.

Obviously, these goals are compatible with the objectives of consumer agencies and consumer legislation. While the bureaus lack judicial authority to prosecute grievances, their practical powers of persuasion towards reputable business may be sufficient to adjust a problem.

Legislation in Washington has produced a consumer protection law which permits the Consumer Protection Division of the attorney general's office to process consumer complaints either by means of adjustment and satisfaction or, if necessary, by litigation.

Specific areas of consumer protection activities in Washington have included employment agencies, door-to-door selling, installment contracts, and the like.

The plight of the consumer has been recognized by most of the states and accordingly they have enacted wide sweeping legislation not only to prohibit deceptive and unconscionable practices but also to provide effective means of adjusting problems, punishing violators, and redressing grievances. More importantly, however, the states through their various agencies have recognized the need to educate the consuming public.

Chapter III
SUMMARY OF MISCELLANEOUS STATE PROVISIONS

The Uniform Consumer Credit Code (U.C.C.C.)

The Uniform Consumer Code, although thus far adopted only in the states of Oklahoma, Colorado, Utah, Indiana, Idaho, Wyoming and Kansas, provides a wide range of consumer protection devices. These devices are detailed in the U.C.C.C.'s six different articles: general provisions, credit sales (including home solicitation), loans, insurance, remedies and administration.

Although only seven states have adopted the entire U.C.C.C., other states have enacted as law a section of the Code. For example, the Code's provisions relating to home solicitation sales have been largely followed in statutes adopted by New York, Florida, Missouri, Maine and Virginia.

The Consumer Credit Code contains certain exclusions, and restrictions as to its territorial applicability. It provides consumer protection via:

- limits on maximum interest charges for a sale; closing costs and official taxes; limits on delinquency charges, deferral charges, service charge, refinancing charge; right of prepayment and rebates upon prepayment.

- disclosure and advertising requirements on sales.

- limits on agreements and practices used in sales such as multiple agreements, negotiable instruments, assignees, liability, security, cross-collateral, referral sales, attorney's fees, default charges and confess judgments.

- allows cancellations of home solicitation sale within 3 days; provides for statement of buyer's rights, restoration of tendered payment, and return of goods.

- limits rate of charge on loans; provides for disclosure and advertising of loans and regulates practices associated with loans such as balloon payments, assignment of earnings; default charges.

- allows special supervised loans at greater than maximum interest rate.

- contains safeguards for insurance provided in relation to a consumer credit sale, loan or lease.

- provides remedies and provisions for deficiency judgments, garnishment, extortionary extensions of credit, unconscionability, voidness, civil liability for disclosure violations, rescission, and refunds.

- allows criminal penalties for willful violations and disclosure violations.

UNFAIR TRADE PRACTICESs

Many of the states have adopted both general fair trade Practice statutes and insurance trade practice statutes.

The Uniform Deceptive Trade Practices Act as enacted by Hawaii, Georgia, Florida, Idaho and Illinois, provides that the following are prohibited deceptive trade practices:

1. Passing off goods and services as those of another;

2. Causing likelihood of confusion or of misunderstanding as to the source, sponsorship, approval or certification of goods and services;

3. Causing likelihood of confusion or of misunderstanding as to affiliation, connection, or association with, or certification by another;

4. Using deceptive representations of geographic origin;

5. Representing that goods or services have sponsorship, approval, characteristics, ingredients, uses, benefits, or quantities that they do not have or that a person has an approval, status affiliation, or connection that he does not have;

6. Representing that goods are original or new if they are deteriorated, altered, reconditioned, reclaimed, used or second-hand;

7. Representing that goods or services are of a particular standard, quality, or grade, or that goods are of a particular style, or model, if they are of another;

8. Disparaging the goods, services, or business of another by false or misleading representations of fact;

9. Advertising goods with intent not to sell them as advertised;

10. Advertising goods or services with intent not to supply expectable public demand, unless the advertisement discloses a limited quantity;

11. Making false or misleading statements concerning the reasons for, existence of, or amounts of price reductions;

12. Engaging in any other conduct which similarly creates a likelihood of confusion or misunderstanding.

In 1971 the National Commissioners on Uniform State Laws issued a "Uniform Consumer Sales Practice Act." This proposed Uniform Act would outlaw eleven types of deceptive consumer sales practices and six types of unconscionable consumer sales practices. It would also establish a central state "Enforcing Authority" with power to enforce the Act, hold hearings and issue rules. Besides providing numerous remedial powers, the Act also adopts provisions which grant individuals private remedies and set out class action standards.

Several states have enacted consumer fraud legislation: Illinois, Missouri, and New Jersey. The acts generally prohibit deception in connection with the sale or advertisement of any merchandise.

Retail Installment Sales Act

At least twenty-six states (California, Connecticut, Delaware, Georgia, Hawaii, Indiana, Kansas, Louisiana, Maryland, Massachusetts, Mississippi, Montana, Nebraska, Nevada, New Hampshire, New Jersey, New Mexico, New York, North Dakota, Ohio, Oregon, Pennsylvania, Tennessee, Texas, Vermont, Washington; for citation to particular statutory provisions, see Appendix A). Most of these laws are similar, although some states have more extensive provisions. Texas, Ohio, Georgia and Vermont have just a basic retail installment contract act although even these states have slight variations.

Some states, like California, include "prohibited contractual provisions" as part of their retail installment sales act. The prohibited contractual provisions relate to a buyer's waiver of a claim or defense or right of action, acceleration of maturity of debt, power of attorney, entry to premises for repossession, and relief from liability for buyer's remedies.

States such as New Jersey and Vermont require that each sales finance company be licensed by the state after making application, payment of fee, and undergoing an investigation to determine if the "financial responsibility, experience, character, and general fitness of the applicant are such to warrant belief that the business will be operated honestly, fairly and efficiently and not in violation of the terms of this chapter or other provisions of law . . ." In addition, New Jersey has provisions relating to prepayment, transfer or assignments, acceleration clauses, and additional charges.

Truth in Lending Laws

At least ten states have adopted some form of truth in lending provisions: Connecticut, Hawaii, Illinois, Kansas, Kentucky. Maine, Massachusetts, New Jersey, Rhode Island, Tennessee, New York repealed its truth in lending statute in 1969. Often, truth in lending provisions of other states exist in miscellaneously classified statutes or under a different name, such as motor vehicle time sales disclosure.

Massachusetts, Kansas and Connecticut all have an identical law which prescribes the determination of what constitutes the finance charge, limits its amount, requires conspicuous disclosure of the charge, permits buyer rescission within 3 days after sale, exempts certain transactions from disclosure requirements, and allows the State Consumer Credit Commission to promulgate rules and regulations to effectuate this law.

Illinois law is not as extensive as those of these three states. Illinois statutes provide for a long list of items to be disclosed in creating a consumer installment loan. Neither penalties nor specific provisions for administrative enforcement are found in the statutes, but they do give the administrative body the authority to promulgate rules. Rhode Island has a similar procedure.

Unsolicited Goods

At least eighteen states (Delaware, Hawaii, Kansas, Maine, Michigan, Minnesota, Missouri, Montana, Nebraska, Nevada, New Jersey, New York, Oklahoma, Oregon, Pennsylvania, Washington, West Virginia, Wisconsin (see Appendix A for particular statutory provisions) now have some provision protecting the consumer when unsolicited goods are involved. Most of the statutes follow the same theme: the unsolicited goods can be rejected, accepted or treated as a gift.

57

Chapter IV

INTELLIGENT BUYING

Many of the states which responded to the inquiry this writer made supplied informational pamphlets listing various areas in which consumers could protect themselves in buying and financing purchases. The following is a list, some with explanation, of the most prevalent areas of consumer pitfalls.

Don't buy in haste.

Don't be high-pressured by a slick salesman.

Don't be fooled by "golden opportunity," "once in a life-time" bargains.

Don't pay a door-to-door salesman before checking his credentials and identification.

Don't permit a household appliance, radio, or TV set to be taken from your home for repairs without first getting a written estimate of probable repair cost.

Don't pay for a neighbor's package unless requested to do so.

Don't deal with fly-by-night merchants.

Don't be bargain-blind.

Don't accept or rely on oral promises.

Don't make unrealistic financial commitments.

Don't allow a door-to-door salesman to leave merchandise with you on approval.

Don't accept an incomplete bill for your merchandise.

The State of California instructs its consumers to listen for these words of warning:

You have won a free . . . .

I am not a salesman.

Only a few people are getting this special deal.

This is your last chance -- I will not be in the neighborhood again.

This low-priced advertised special is not for you, you want this expensive one.

Not only do you get these books, but you also get . . . . . .

It will only cost you the price of one package of cigarettes a day.

This is a great item, it is guaranteed for life.

I am in a contest -- one more order and I will win.

These statements should be an immediate warning to the consumer that the transaction may not be all that it is supposed to be. Upon hearing them or similar promises or representations the consumer's red light of caution should begin to flash.

Ohio has published and distributes a "Consumer Survival Manual." That manual gives the consumer of average intelligence a plan of operation in making any purchases. The consumer is instructed to read and understand all papers before signing them. He is told to buy only from reputable businessmen and to be skeptical of many advertising claims. He is advised to take his time in making any purchase and to investigate not only the product, but also the seller. A seller's reputation may be checked through the better business bureau, chamber of commerce, or the consumer fraud and crimes section of the state's attorney general's office.

Areas of prime concern to the Ohio manual are the "bait and switch" selling tactics, the sympathy approach to selling, home improvement and repair frauds, chain merchandising schemes, warranties and guarrantees, door-to-door salesmen, free gifts for buying, phony health products, money making at home ideas, and referral sales frauds.

Ohio has reported that its citizens are taken for more than $300,000,000 each year through inferior products, overpricing, exhorbitantly high interest rates, unneeded products or services, and fraudulent practices. The amount is staggering to the imagination when considered in the light of fifty-two states.

New York, too, spends considerable time and money in trying to educate its consumers in buying techniques. In response to this writer's inquiry of New York, several very complete lists of wise buying procedures were supplied. The following are those procedures recommended in the particular areas specified and reprinted with permission of the New York State's attorney general's office.

HOME IMPROVEMENTS

1.   Get estimates from several contractors in writing.

2.   Check the reliability of the contractor you want to use with local merchants and others for whom he has done work.

3.   Check with local authorities regarding licensing of home

contractors, and if mandatory in your area, ask to see his license before signing a contract.

4. Have your contract dated and in writing, carefully spelling out a description of the work to be done, and including both starting and completion dates.

5. Be wary of the salesman or contractor who asks you to pay in advance, or to pay cash, instead of in the usual manner by check or money order on completion, or in installments as the contract specifies.

6. Do not sign a completion certificate unless the work is completed to your satisfaction.

7. Be certain that the contractor will clean up when the job is finished.

8. If there is a guarantee, be sure that is spells out details clearly, including the period for which the guarantee will be in effect.

9. Check with local authorities regarding a law permitting you to cancel a contract by notifying the contractor, under certain conditions.

10. Make certain that the contract includes in writing all promises made by the salesman.

11. If you need to borrow money to pay for the work, check first with your bank or other reputable financing agencies before you contract for work to be done.

12. Discuss the contract with your attorney before signing.

GUARANTEE

1. Always put it in writing -- accept <u>no</u> verbal promises.

2. How will the guarantee be kept? -- (Will repairs be made on damaged parts, will broken parts be replaced, will refunds be made for ineffective parts, is labor for repairs included?).

3. Who is making the guarantee -- the seller or the manufacturer? (Make sure you return the manufacturer's guarantee card -- if one is included).

4. The person making the guarantee is responsible for the true description of the product.

5. Lifetime guarantee must clarify -- whose lifetime -- product's or owner's?

6. 50% savings guarantees -- must make provisions for what will happen if this amount is not saved, and, if there are time limits involved, just what they are.

7. Satisfaction or money back guarantees -- are expected to promptly return the full purchase price -- unless stated otherwise in the guarantee.

8. Unconditionally guaranteed products -- which prove to be defective in any way, are expected to be replaced, repaired, or full purchase price refunded, and, in addition, must clearly state the time limit involved.

9. "Guaranteed" -- products will be regarded to be the same as unconditionally guaranteed, fulfilling the same conditions as well.

10. Pro rata guarantees -- must be clearly described, and based on a conspicuously placed price, since these vary according to product depreciation.

CONSUMER BUYING RIGHTS

1. No advertiser or seller can engage in the practice of discouraging the purchaser of the advertised product as part of a bait or scheme to sell another product. It is illegal in New York State under the General Business Law, Section 396.

2. Deal only with honest dealers who provide both the opportunity to buy the advertised merchandise and salesmen whose representations for the products are the same as those made in the advertisements.

3. Deal with the store which has a large stock of the advertised article.

4. Be aware that although the reputable merchant may show the customer other goods of the same kind at a higher price, he does not deliverately resist selling the advertised article, nor does he place unnecessary and untrue obstacles to deter the customer from purchasing the item.

GOOD HEALTH

1. Avoid "door bell" doctors, doctors promising quick answers and cures, and those making medical and biological diagnosis through the mails.

2. Avoid health lecturers whose "pitches" are made in small hotel rooms, admission free, with the end result being a product for sale.

3. Make sure your doctor has academic training in his field, his degree from a reputable institution, is listed in high standard professional directories, and belongs to well qualified medical organizations.

4. Do not place reliance upon medical testimonials or case histories used in advertising to promote "miraculous cures."

5. Do not purchase "quick cure" remedies, they may be dangerous to health and life when used with or without supervision. They are often worthless for the purposes for which they are intended, and they can be detrimental to actual conditions for which they are offered, sometimes even causing irreparable damage.

6. Above all, see a competent and reputable doctor when worried about your health, particularly in cases involving persistent and recurring disorders.

BUYING A USED CAR

1. Carefully inspect the car's interior and exterior -- look for signs of wear and age in:

a. broken seats, torn upholstery and pedal pads;
b. broken or ill-fitting doors and windows;
c. poorly operating brake pedal;
d. oily "scum" in radiator area;
e. rust and dampness under floor mats;
f. repainted areas along body sides.

2. Take your car for a road test -- listen for: squeaks, knocks, rattles, and unusual noises.
Look for: smooth start; tight, even steering; quick engine pickup; cool radiator (no overheating); etc.

3. Take the car to a competent and reputable mechanic for a thorough checkup.

4. Be wary of low mileage on an older car. (A good mechanic can tell if the mileage has been set back -- a practice illegal in New York State.)

5. Understand the purchase contract, thoroughly. Don't sign one with blank spaces, make sure you have a copy, and question anything you don't understand.

6. Be certain that all verbal promises are put in writing.

7. If you buy on credit, make certain you know the full purchase price of the car -- and what the interest will be.

8. Be sure, when you answer an advertisement, you see the car which was advertised -- don't be switched to a newer, fancier, higher-priced model.

9. Above all, buy from locally established or well-recommended dealers who have earned the fine reputation that they enjoy.

BUYING AN AIR CONDITIONER

1. Buy from an honest dealer -- in your community, or one highly recommended and well established.

2. Make sure you get the total price -- including delivery, installation, warranty, etc.

3. Make sure all verbal promises are put in writing.

4. See that the guarantee is specific -- spelling out how long it will be effective, and who will honor it.

5. If there is a service contract -- find out if it is at an extra cost, who will provide the service, and exactly what is provided.

6. Don't sign any agreement you do not thoroughly understand.

7. If possible -- ask to see the unit you plan to buy demonstrated, if not, study the instruction manual, so that you know how to use it.

8. Don't be lured into the store with promises of low prices -- only to be switched to a higher priced model -- the advertised model being unobtainable (sold out, not in stock, etc.).

9. When considering repair of a unit:
   a. Get a written itemized estimate (before and after the actual work is done);
   b. Make sure (by checking with another company) that removal of the unit is essential for its repair;
   c. Beware of excessive prices for parts and labor.

HOW TO SPOT WORK-AT-HOME GYPS

1. Be wary of large-profit offers for little or no work.

2. The "for sale" material is not employment, but a product.

3. The investment required is yours (time and money).

4. No salary is ever given by the company.

5. No names are provided for you to check with others, for the benefit of their experience.

6. No leads or market for your product is provided.

LEGISLATION COVERING UNORDERED MERCHANDISE

"Any person receiving unsolicited goods, wares, or

65

merchandise offerd for sale, but not actually requested or ordered by him orally or in writing, shall be entitled to consider such goods, wares, or merchandise an unconditional gift, and he may use or dispose of the same as he sees fit without any obligation on his part to the sender."

Don't be pressured to pay, by companies who make a practice of mailing unordered merchandise on a "trial basis" in hopes that you will keep it, rather than go through the trouble involved in making a return.

THE ALERT CONSUMER

1. Ask to see the credentials of any sales representative who calls at your door.

2. Check the sales price of services or merchandise with your local merchant.

3. Read and understand everything before you sign a contract:
   a. Did you read the small print?
   b. Is guarantee specific?
   c. Are all blank spaces filled in?
   d. Are all charges itemized?
   e. Are all promises in writing?
   f. Do you have a copy?

4. Where you do not understand the terms of a sales contract, see a lawyer.

5. If the sales price does not include installation and delivery, and you want them included, have the salesman put it in writing in the contract, specifying the type of service, the period during which it will be performed, and the actual date of delivery.

6. Never permit merchandise to be left with you on an "on approval" receipt. The salesman may not return, and you may find yourself billed for an article you neither needed or wanted.

7. Beware of legal "double talk" -- remember that you just can't get something for nothing!

66

8. If you buy something from a salesman at the door, pay him with a check made out to the company rather than with cash.

9. Purchases bought on the installment plan from a salesman at the door may now be thought over, and canceled (in writing) within three days after signing the initial agreement.

OTHER HINTS -- AVOID DEALERS & MANUFACTURERS WHO FAIL TO:

1. Give prompt attention to complaints -- have no system for receiving, routing, or handling them and evade specific questions along these lines.

2. Honor the guarantee.

3. Write the guarantee in terms which are generally understandable.

4. Replace a "lemon" with a new appliance or refund the purchase price.

5. Take satisfactory direct action -- thereby causing the consumer to pay excessive costs for service and labor in order to repair the appliance.

6. Make necessary repairs -- because parts are not readily available, or because of a manufacturer's delay in authorizing a replacement part, sometimes resulting in spoilage (freezers, etc.).

7. Improve or correct design defects causing repeated breakdown.

8. Provide a free, nominal, or easy way for consumer to return appliances in cases of breakdown.

9. Provide experienced and skilled servicemen whose training is up to date on the latest models.

FOR THOSE DOOR-TO-DOOR SALES

1. Check the salesman's identification -- make sure he rep-

resents the company he claims he does.

2. Make sure the firm is reliable -- check with others with whom he has dealt.

3. Don't be pressured into making an immediate purchase -- compare prices with local merchants and other stores.

4. Know the exact terms and conditions of the sale -- don't sign any agreement you do not understand.

5. Before you sign any contract make sure:
   a. the name and address of the firm and salesman are printed on it;
   b. it has no blank spaces;
   c. all verbal promises which were made are so specified in the contract;
   d. it is specific as to how payments are to be made, delivery date, etc.;
   e. you know the nature of the guarantee (if any).

6. You don't pay cash to a salesman -- pay your bill by check or money order, made out to the company.

7. You have a copy of the contract.

8. Remember that, effective September 1, 1970 in New York State, a law was passed, providing for a three-day cooling-off period to permit a purchaser of a retail installment sales contract from a door-to-door salesman to think over his purchase, change his mind, and cancel the contract, if he chooses, notifying the company in writing within three days of the initial agreement.

Chapter V *Cases*

THE CONSUMER AND FRANCHISING

The franchise system, having experienced a tremendous growth in a relatively short period of time, is now the subject of close scrutiny, both legislative and judicial. Basic to all franchise relationships is the temendous disparity of bargaining position which exists between the franchisor and the consumer who seeks to become a franchisee.

The right of the franchisor to terminate or fail to renew a contract for no apparent reason is but one example of the perils under which a franchisee operates. Should a franchisor have unrestricted freedom to decline renewal of the franchise? One authority in the field states:

> "While the actual term of a franchise can be set for any period, ultimately the time will arrive for renewal of the franchise. A few agreements give the franchisee an exclusive option to renew. More frequently renewal is either dependent on the agreement of both parties or in the sole discretion of the franchisor. Whatever the original term of the franchise, any franchisee who has survived all other hazards will have built up some equity in the business. That equity will be in jeopardy if the franchisor has unrestricted freedom to decline renewal of the franchise." (Harold Brown, Franchising: Trap for the Trusting, Little Brown and Co., 1970, p. 26.)

Recent years have seen the growth of a body of law concerning franchise agreements. To date, there are several states which are considering fair franchising act, and there is federal legislation regulating certain aspects of automobile dealer franchise agreements with manufacturers. 15 U.S.C.A. 1221 et seq. The Dealer's Day in Court Act, as it is called, was the culmination of numerous judicial decisions respecting the rights and obligations of automobile dealers and their manufacturers. While there is federal legislation being considered with regard to the remaining franchise arrangements (Fairness in Franchising Act, S. 1967), there is currently no federal legislation to govern

69

the operation of franchise agreements outside of the automobile industry.

Basically, the Dealer's Day in Court Act imposes a "good faith" limitation on each and every franchise agreement entered into between a manufacturer and an automotive dealer. While the Dealer's Day in Court Act does not govern other franchise problems, some of the rationale which went into the creation of the act, and the cases which were decided in the automotive industry prior to the enactment of that act are helpful in understanding franchise problems.

Once the courts decided that a franchise agreement was a valid contract, Buggs v. Ford Motor Company, 113 F. 2d 618 (1940), the majority of decisions which followed thereafter found the courts refusing to impose limitation of good faith on the power of the manufacturer to terminate the relationship. Bushwick-Decatur Motors, Inc. v. Ford Motor Company, 116 F. 2d 675 (1940); Martin v. Ford Motor Company, 93 F. Supp. 920 (1950).

Once, however, the courts began to recognize the disparity of bargaining position existing between the manufacturers and the dealers, they began in certain instances to impose that limitation of good faith. Patterson-Pope Motor Company v. Ford Motor Company, 16 S. E. 2d 877 (1941); Kane v. Chrysler Corporation, 80 F. Supp. 360 (1948).

In the Patterson-Pope case, the plaintiff-dealer was induced to make a large investment in physical plant and equipment, only to have the Ford Motor Company cancel the franchise eleven months after its inception. The court held that the dealer had the right to believe and to act on the assumption that the contract was being offered by the manufacturer in good faith and that the parties contemplated extended performance which would result in the mutual profit of both.

When a franchise agreement terminates, whether it be a refusal to renew, or a termination of a relationship existing without a written contract, the end result is a refusal by the franchisor to deal further with the franchisee. Termination and/or the failure to renew the franchise agreement are forms of a "refusual to deal." Simpson v. Union Oil Company, 377 U.S. 13 (1964).

When this refusal to deal is the result of a lack of good faith, or an unlawful purpose, the end result to the dealer is a forfeiture of his time and efforts and the expenditures that he has incurred while developing and promoting the manufacturer's products. The result, then, in these cases, is unconscionable and

the fact that the contract provides for termination does not negate
the drastic results on the dealer terminated.

> "Nor is it any answer to contend, as a freedom
> of contract theory exponent might, that where the
> parties have freely allocated the risks, the termin-
> ated party should live with the bargain he has made
> and not be the beneficiary of special judicial relief.
> Such medieval notions of justice or fairness are no
> longer justifiable, even if the enterprisers have
> equal bargaining power and ability.
>
> At least some consideration ought to be given to
> the relative burdens imposed on each of the parties
> by enforcing or refusing to enforce the termination
> provision at that time." (Ernest Gellhorn, "Limi-
> tations on Contract Termination Rights -- Fran-
> chise Cancellations," Duke Law Journal, vol. 1967,
> no. 3.)

As early as 1931, the courts began to impose the good faith
provision on termination options, and to discount the freedom of
contract theory. J. R. Watkins Co. v. Rich, et al., 235 N.W. 845
(1931). In cases not involving automobile dealers decided after
the Dealer's Day in Court Act had been passed, the courts began
applying good faith determination provisions of franchises existing between manufacturers and dealers other than automotive.
Gaines W. Harrison & Son, Inc. v. J. I. Case Company, 180 Fed.
Supp. 243 (1960).

The question then arises as to what is meant by good faith.
Good faith as defined by federal legislation means:

> "the duty of each party to any franchise, and
> all officers, employees, or agents thereof to act in
> a fair and equitable manner toward each other so as
> to guarantee the one party freedom from coertion,
> intimidation, or threats of coertion or intimidation
> from the other party; provided, That recom-
> mendation, endorsement, expostion, persuasion,
> urging or argument shall not be deemed to consti-
> tute a lack of good faith." 15 U.S. C.A. Section 1221
> (e).

A good number of the automotive cases have arisen under
alleged arbitrary application of minimum sales requirements.
For example, Madsen v. Chrysler Corp., 261 F. Supp. 488 (1966).
In areas other than automobile dealers, the courts have held that
a refusal to deal would be illegal if done for the purpose of

pursuing a monopoly, Eastman Co. v. Southern Photo Co., 273 U.S. 359 (1927); if done as a result of a conspiracy between the franchisor and franchisees, United States v. General Motors Corp., et al. 384 U.S. 127 (1966); if done for the purpose of illegally promoting territorial or customer allocation arrangements, United States v. Arnold, Schwinn & Co., 388 U.S. 350 (1967); White Motor Co. v. United States, 372 U.S. 253 (1963).

The court in U.S. v. Arnold, Schwinn & Co., supra, cited Susser v. Carvel Corp. 206 F. Supp. 636, 640.

> The franchise method of operation has the advantage, from the standpoint of our American system of competitive economy, of enabling numerous groups of individuals with small capital to become entrepreneurs -- If our economy had not developed that system of operation, these individuals would have turned out to have been merely employees. The franchise system creates a class of independent businessmen, it provides the public with an opportunity to get a uniform product at numerous points of sale from small independent contractors, rather than from employees of a vast chain.

The court further said:

> Indiscriminate invalidation of franchising arrangements would eliminate their creative contributions to competition and force suppliers to abandon franchising and integrate forward to the detriment of small business.

The end result of franchise terminations may be a reduction in competition. As such the motive, the intent, and the purpose behind a franchisor's refusal to deal with the franchisee is unlawful, is not in good faith, and cannot be sustained.

In reviewing the "rule of reason" of the Sherman Act, the court in White Motor Company v. United States, supra, cited Chicago Board of Trade v. United States, 246 U.S. 231, 238.

> "Every agreement concerning trade, every regulation of trade, restrains. To bind, to restrain, is of their very essence. The true test of legality is whether the restraint imposed is such as merely regulate and perhaps thereby promotes competition or whether it is such as may suppress or even destroy competition."

The failure to renew alone may be actionable under the current trend of the law.

72

The Fairness in Franchising Act, presented to the United States Senate, states that it shall be a violation of that act for any franchisor to terminate, cancel, or fail to renew a franchise except for good cause. Good cause for failing to renew is:

> (a) "failure by the franchisee to substantially comply with those requirements imposed upon by the franchise which requirements are both essential and reasonable, or
>
> (b) "use of bad faith by the franchisee in carrying out the terms of the franchise."

This act, then, shifts the burden of proof from the franchisee of showing bad faith by the franchisor, to the franchisor who now must show good faith in refusing to continue the relationship.

Realistic state legislation, Massachusets Legislature (H.2279) continued the trend. Section f. thereof provides:

> f. "Anything to the contrary notwithstanding, it shall be unlawful for the franchisor or subfranchisor to fail to renew a franchise on terms then equally available to all franchisees, to terminate a franchise, or to restrict the transfer of a franchise, unless the franchisee received fair and reasonable compensation for the value of the franchise including its good-will and his contribution to the particular franchise either as a going business (unless the business shall have been terminated without the substantial fault of the franchisor or subfranchisor) or at liquidation value (in the absence of such substantial fault), due weight to be given to such franchise fees as the franchisee may have paid for the franchise. In any case, the consent of the franchisor shall not be unreasonably withheld."

The comment to that section is quite enlightening.

> "COMMENT. These restrictions on the right of renewal, termination, and transfer are designed to assure to the franchisee the value of his equity and goodwill in his business. In substance, franchisors are required to make good on their universal promise that the franchisee is purchasing and developing a "business of your own."

Delaware recently enacted legislation closely resembling the Massachusetts act and it is conceivable that the majority of states will adopt such realistic legislation in the near future.

Uniform legislation has been presented to the American Trade Association Managers which legislation would insure fair and equitable treatment of franchisees as sought by this particular plaintiff in this particular case.

Since the judiciary for the most part has not had the appropriate legislation to rely on in granting franchisees relief from improper treatment by their franchisors, several unique theories have been established upon which the needed relief could be granted.

The theories of fraud, antitrust violations, and even security regulation have been invoked by various state courts and the National Labor Relations Board in protecting franchisees.

Behind each one of these, perhaps, tenuous arguments is the effort of the courts to do justice and protect the equity the franchisee has built up, the time and effort he had devoted and reasonably compensate him for his misplaced trust and confidence reposed in the franchisor.

Although courts have traditionally refused to issue a decree enforcing a contractual relationship upon two parties where it is incumbent upon the parties to devote their best efforts in distributing a product, Bach v. Friedan Calculating Machine Company, 155 F. 2d 361 (1946), there have been several cases in which the court has disregarded that theory and imposed mandatory injunctions on the defendant.

> "We note that the Sixth Circuit, in a case involving a somewhat similar franchise agreement, denied an injunction against interference with the franchise because the Court thought it would be too difficult to enforce, Bach v. Frieden Calculating Machine Company. Any difficulty of enforcement here does not impress us. All the defendant need do is to refrain from acting in bad faith, as it has presumably so refrained during most -- if not all -- of the 29 years this franchise has existed." Bateman v. Ford Motor Company, 302 F. 2d 63, 67 (1962).

Similar injunctions were granted Madsen v. Chrysler Corporation, supra, and Swartz v. Chrysler Corporation, 297 F. Supp. 834 (1969).

In Hoffman Candy and Ice Cream Co. v. Dept. of Liquor of the State of Ohio, et al., 154 Ohio St. 357 (1930), Justice Malthias wrote an astute opinion in dissenting with the majority who refused to grant a mandatory injunction requiring the parties to deal together in the future.

> "At common law a principal may discharge his agent even though there is a contract that such agency should continue for a definite period of time. In cases where resulting damages might have been collected by an action at law, specific performance is denied, but in a situation such as presented in this case, equitable relief should be awarded.

> "This is not a question of mere personal service. Plaintiff, at considerable expense, remodeled its store and devoted a portion of its space and the services of its employees to the performance of the duties prescribed by the terms of the contract entered into with the Dept. of Liquor Control. The carrying out of the decree of specific performance in this case does not represent any of the difficulties which lead courts in the cases cited in the majority of opinion to refuse relief."

In many of the cases decided under the Dealer's Day in Court Act, the courts have granted preliminary injunctions and there seems to be no difficulty in the parties continuing their relationship while these cases pend for a number of years.

There are numerous areas of franchising which may involve violation of federal statutes, primarily of the antitrust nature. While all of these cannot be examined, it is important to mention two of these as they most directly affect a consumer who is seeking to enter into a franchise relationship.

The first of these areas is the promise of a franchisor that the franchisee will be granted an exclusive territory in which to operate. Territory exclusivity has been taken to be a per se violation of the antitrust laws. That is, the mere granting of an exclusive territory alone is proof that the relationship is one that is in restraint of trade. While a franchisor may agree that he will not compete with his franchisee within a certain geographical area, he cannot prohibit other franchisees from so competing. In an effort to grant the franchise some degree of exclusivity, the franchisor may lawfully agree that he will not appoint another franchisee in the same area, but he cannot assure the franchisee that there will be no competition from other franchisees who are headquartered in a close geographic area.

The second area which the consumer should watch in entering into a franchise agreement is a requirement that he purchase all products, supplies, and the like from the franchisor. These provisions, known as tying agreements, are illegal under the antitrust laws. The leading case in this area is <u>Siegal et al. v. Chicken Delight, Inc.</u>, 448 F. 2d 43 (1971).

The United States Court of Appeals, Ninth Circuit, in hearing and determining that case held that the sale of a franchise license with attendant rights to operate a business in the prescribed manner and to benefit from the good will of the trade name does not require a forced sale by the franchisor of some or all of component articles.

The court gave this synopsis of the case. Where a trademark of licensor of several hundred franchisees operating home delivery and pick-up food stores was distinctive and possessed good will and public acceptance unique to it and not enjoyed by other fast food chains, the tying product, the license to use the trademark, possessed sufficient market power to bring within the Sherman Act the franchisees', claim for treble damages for injuries allegedly resulting from the franchisor's standard form franchise agreements requiring the franchisees to purchase essential cooking equipment, dry-mix food items, and trademark-bearing packaging exclusively from the franchisor as a condition to obtaining the trademark license. While the franchisor has some control over the quality and standards of the particular products a franchisor can use, he cannot effectively require the franchisee to purchase the products from him. This, of course, takes some of the very big profits out of the franchising arrangement, and is another step in the long chain of consumer protection.

Without going into any further detail, the consumer who is thinking about entering into a franchise relationship should be aware of the following areas of the agreement which may be in violation of antitrust legislation:

1. Price Control, including minimum and maximum prices;

2. Territorial exclusivity;

3. Restricting the class of customers to whom the franchisee may sell;

4. Restrictions as to the franchisee's source of supplies;

5. Restrictions as to competing merchandise, non-competing merchandise, and even nonrelated merchandise;

6. Inventory controls;

7. Requirements as to physical layout;

8. Requirements as to uniforms;

9. Prescription as to days and hours of business;

10. Restrictive covenant to to compete;

11. Unreasonable provisions as to length of contract and restrictions on sale or transfer;

12. Overbearing provisions as to termination or refusal to renew.
(Harold Brown, Franchising: Trap for the Trusting, p. 65)

FRANCHISE CHECK LIST

1. Be sure to investigate before investing any money or signing any written agreements. Discuss with a lawyer and other franchisees who have been operating in the same general area for at least one year.

2. Carefully examine records and accounts, checking out all operational costs.

3. Check the reliability of the firm, the length of time in business, its accomplishments, the kind of people managing and working for it, and the long range plan of action.

4. Make certain that the product is practical (not a fad or seasonal item) -- priced competitively, packaged attractively, and has wide appeal.

5. See that the sales territory is well defined, has good sales potential and growth possibilities, is an area whose residents have an income which can afford the item being sold,

and carefully survey the competition.

6. The contract should: (a) cover all aspects of the agreement, spelling out in writing all verbal promises made, (b) indicate whether the franchise can be renewed, transferred, or terminated, (c) provide for a specific return merchandise credit policy, (d) indicate if there is a franchise fee -- what it is, (e) how much of an annual sales quota must be met, (f) if the franchisee can have other business interests, (g) if there is a fixed payment each year, etc.

7. Make sure that training assistance, manuals, sales aides, purchasing guides, and advertising assistance are provided.

Chapter VI

HISTORY OF CONSUMERISM

As illustrated in the Introduction, consumerism is fast becoming a watchword of our times. Caveat emptor no longer is applicable. Public reaction to and indignation with shoddy and fraudulent consumer practices has led to the initiation of legislation and the creation of numerous consumer protection agencies.

Earliest consumer activities in the United States involved attempts at assuring quality in foods. The entire country was shocked out of its complacency by Upton Sinclair's The Jungle. This expose of the meat packing industry led to the first food and drug legislation.

In 1938 Congress enacted the Wheeler-Lea amendment to the Federal Trade Commission Act of 1914. This act expanded the area in which the Federal Trade Commission could protect consumers by eliminating the need to establish that the act complained of had limited competition, as was previously required.

Through the years the jurisdiction of other federal agencies has been expanded, and extensive federal legislation has been enacted for consumer protection. Among the later ones are Truth-in-Securities, Truth-in-Lending and Truth-in-Packaging legislation.

Extensive state legislation has been enacted contemporaneously with federal legislation. Each of the state laws seeks to eliminate "unfair or deceptive acts" or practices in many areas. These laws will be examined in detail later.

Among the federal agencies which have been established or expanded to aid the consumer are the Interstate Commerce Commission, the Utilities and Transportation Commission, the Food and Drug Administration, the Department of Social and Health Services, the Department of Agriculture, the Securities and Exchange Commission, the Federal Trade Commission, and advisory groups to the President on consumer affairs.

The judiciary, too, has and is taking an active part in consumerism. Of course, the courts must have the basic tools with which to work -- statutory enactments -- but a vast body of law is developing in the courts. An important tool which the courts have recently invoked is Section 2-302 of the Uniform Commercial

Code. That uniform piece of legislation has been adopted by all the states except Louisiana and, in general, governs most consumer transactions.

Section 2-302 permits a court to declare that a particular clause or an entire contract is unconscionable and results in oppression or unfair surprise to a consumer. There have been four very recent cases which have applied the theory of Section 2-302 and have resulted in decisions helpful to the cause of consumerism.

In American Home Improvement, Inc. v. MacIver, 201 A. 2d 886, the court refused to enforce a contract because the value of actual services rendered to a consumer was far below the contract price. Only $959 of a total price of $2,568 was representative of actual services rendered.

A referral sales program whereby color televisions were sold to consumers who would refer other customers for a commission gave rise to a second case. Upon delivery of the goods, the contracts were immediately discounted. A New York court hearing that case, captioned State by Lefkovitz v. ITM, Inc., 275 NYS 2d 303, held that the contracts were unconscionable under Section 2-302 of the Uniform Commercial Code and thereby laid to rest the doctrine of caveat emptor.

In Frosttifish Corporation v. Reynoso, 274 NYS 2d 757, the transaction was held to be unconscionable because the service charge almost equaled the price of the goods sold.

The New York court held:

"It is normally stated that the parties are free to make whatever contracts they please so long as there is no fraud or illegality --

However, it is the apparent intent of the Uniform Commercial Code to modify this general rule by giving the courts power to police explicitly against the contracts or clauses which they find to be unconscionable. The principle is one of the prevention of oppression and unfair surprise."

In Williams v. Walker-Thomas Furniture Co., 350 F. 2d 445, a District of Columbia court refused to enforce a contract which provided that goods purchased earlier from the same seller remained as security for later purchases. A default on the new debt could result in the consumer having to surrender all the goods he purchased from that seller even though some had actually been paid for in full. Such a contract is unconscionable and, hence, unenforceable.

The doctrine of <u>caveat</u> <u>emptor</u> is, therefore, slowly but surely being eliminated by operation of the courts, statutory enactments and administrative agencies. A consumer no longer knows just what he is buying or from whom he is buying. Certainly consumers lack the technical knowledge to be able to ascertain the quality of the products they buy. Without aid and assistance, the consumer in today's complicated market place would be at the mercy of the vendor.

The doctrine of <u>caveat</u> <u>emptor</u> has been traditionally applied between a lessor and a lessee. Now, however, an expanding number of states have changed the traditional rule to include what amounts to an implied warranty of habitability flowing from the lessor to the lessee.

A recent Iowa case held that a tenant is entitled to a habitable dwelling, free from latent defects and material housing code violations. These warranties are to be given either orally or in written form and can be included in the written lease of the dwelling house, condominium or apartment. A breach of the implied warranty of habitability occurs, according to the Iowa court, when any of the following factors appear:

1. The alleged defects violate building codes, ordinances, or regulations;

2. The deficiency or defect has a negative effect on safety and sanitation;

3. The defect has persisted for an unreasonable length of time;

4. The amount of rent does not justify less than habitable conditions;

5. The tenant did not voluntarily, knowingly and intelligently waive the defects;

6. The defects and deficiencies did not result from abnormal, unusual, or malicious use of the premises by the tenant.

Thus, it can be seen that caveat emptor, even in this traditional stronghold of the doctrine, is dwindling in importance. The situation of landlord-tenant is not the only area where the courts and legislatures have ventured to relegate the doctrine of caveat emptor to a minor role.

The State of Ohio has, for example, enacted a home solicitation sales act which went into effect on January 1, 1973. That law applies to all sales, whether cash or financed, where the purchase price is $35.00 or more, when the contract is signed in the buyer's home.

The law provides that the buyer has the right to cancel the contract by giving written notice to the seller, to be delivered or mailed not later than midnight of the third business day after and not including the day the contract was signed. This right of rescission is in addition to that the buyer might have under the Federal Truth-in-Lending law. The following paragraph must appear in the contract.

Buyer's Right to Cancel

You may cancel this agreement or purchase by mailing a written notice to the Seller postmarked no later than midnight of the third business day after the date this agreement was signed. You may use this page as that notice by writing "I hereby cancel" at the bottom and adding your name and address. The notice must be mailed to:

_____
(name and address of seller)

The caption as shown must be centered over the statement and printed in solid capital letters of not less than twelve-point bold-face type. The remaining words of the statement must be in type at least two points larger than the type used in the contract or purchase agreement. The warning must appear conspicuously in the contract and must be adjacent to or above the buyer's signature lines.

Failure to include the above warning on the part of the vendor may result in a fine of up to $1,000.

Thus, consumerism has rapidly expanded from a concern for edible foods to a vast range of consumer-protection legislation and intricate procedures of state and federal agencies. The courts, too, have taken up the cause for consumerism and these trends in legislation and judicial decisions will be explored throughout the remaining chapters of this almanac.

Chapter VII
CONCLUSION

The consumer now possesses the right to safety, the right to be informed, the right to choose, and the right to be heard. These rights which President Johnson forecast in 1964 have come to be. They are granted to the consumer by means of legislation, state consumer protection agencies, and the courts.

The process of consumerism has been slow, but through the combined efforts of the state and federal governments, the consumer has the tools with which to make progress. Many local governments have enacted their own consumer legislation and have added still another protective level to the ever growing pyramid of consumer protection.

With all of the available consumer protection agencies, legislation, and other aids, the consumer can, if he wishes, effectively protect his rights. However, the primary responsibility still lies with the individual consumer. He must be aware of his rights and must know how to process his grievances. No area of consumerism is more important than the education of the everyday buyer. He must know his rights in the market place, he must know how to be an intelligent buyer, and he must be aware of the traps and pitfalls he faces each and every day of his consuming life.

This almanac has been but a mere insight into the rights of consumers and it cannot be overemphasized that each consumer must familiarize himself with his particular state statutes, local ordinances, and available private agencies which can help him to be a wise and effective consumer.

A consumer who seeks to educate himself in the ways of the market place and to acquaint himself with his rights and legal protections will by his own individual efforts make a meaningful contribution to the process of fair and equitable dealings between consumers and merchants.

Appendix A
STATE CONSUMER
STATUTE REFERENCES

ALABAMA (Alabama Code, 1949, recom. 1958, Supp. 1971)

Collection agencies	Title 51 § 492 et seq.
Consumer finance act	5-316 et seq.
Contracts	9- et seq.
Food (adulteration, inspection, standards)	2-303 et seq.
Fraud	7-107 et seq.
Fraudulent conspiracy	14-103
Fraudulent conveyances	20-1 et seq.
Going out of business sale	57-131 et seq.
Itinerant vendors	51-774 et seq.
Licenses	51-450 et seq.
Sales of checks act	5-301 et seq.
Small loan act	5-277 et seq.
Uniform commercial code	7A- et seq.
Weights and measures	2-587 et seq.

ALASKA (Alaska Statutes, 1962, Supp. 1970)

Collection agencies	§08.24 et seq.
False pretenses and frauds	11.20.360 et seq.
Food	17. et seq.
Insurance contracts	21.42.010 et seq.
Insurance trade practices	21.36.210 et seq.
Land sales practices act	34.55.004 et seq.
Retail installment sale act	45.10.010 et seq.
Small loan act	06.20 et seq.
Unfair trade practices	45.45.010 et seq.
Uniform commercial code	45.05.002 et seq.
Weights and measures	45.75.010 et seq.

ARIZONA (Arizona Revised Statutes, 1956, Supp. 1972)

Advertising	Title 44§1481
Collection agencies	32-1001 et seq.
Conspiracy to defraud	3-331
Consumer fraud	44-1521 et seq.
Consumer reporting agencies	44-1691 et seq.
Contracts	44-101 et seq.
Credit cards	13-1071 et seq.
Credit unions	3-501 et seq.
Dairies- labeling, licensing	3-601 et seq.
Eggs-licensing and inspection	3-701 et seq.
Fair trade practices	44-1421 et seq.
	44-1461 et seq.
False representations	13-661
Food	36-901 et seq.
Frauds	44-1481; 3-311 et seq.;
	44-1211 et seq.
Fraudulent conveyances	44-1001 et seq.
Insurance contracts	20-1101 et seq.
Insurance trade practices	20-441 et seq.
Motor vehicle time sale disclosure	44-281 et seq.
Small loan act	6-601 et seq.
Uniform commercial code	44-2201 et seq.
Weights and measures	44-2101 et seq.

ARKANSAS (Arkansas Statutes, 1947, Supp. 1971)

Advertising	§41-1961 et seq., 70-904
Collection agencies	71-2001 et seq.
Consumer Advisory Board	70-903
Credit cards	41-1965 et seq.
Credit unions	67-901 et seq.
Deceptive sales practices	70-906
Food	82-901 et seq.
Frauds, false pretenses	41-1961 et seq.;
	41-1901 et seq.;
	41-1202 et seq.

85

Fraudulent conveyances	68-1301 et seq.
Insurance trade practices	66-3001 et seq.
Itinerant merchants	84-2401 et seq.
Uniform commercial code	85-1-101 et seq.
	68-603 et seq.;
Usury	68-603 et seq.;
	Const. Art. 19 Sec. 13
Weights and measures	78-201 et séq.

CALIFORNIA (California Annotated Code, Supp. 1973)

Advertising	Bus & Prof. 17530 et seq.
Collection agencies	Bus & Prof. 6850 et seq.
Credit cards	Civil 1718 et seq.;
	Penal 484a, 502.7
Credit sales	Civil 1801 et seq.
Credit unions	Fin 14000 et seq.
Consumer Affairs act	Bus & Prof. 300 et seq.
Consumer counsel office	Govt. 12050 et seq.
Consumer credit reporting agency	Civil 1750 et seq.
Consumer legal remedies	Civil 1750 et seq.
Consumer warranty protection	Civil 1790 et seq.
Contracts	Civil 1588 et seq.
Dance studio contracts	Civil 1812.50 et seq.
Fraud	Civil 1709
Fraudulent conveyances	Civil 3439 et seq.
Health studio contracts	Civil 1812.80 et seq.
Insurance contracts	Insur. 100 et seq.
Pure Drug Act	Health & Saf. 26200 et seq.
Pure Food Act	Health & Saf. 26450 et seq.
Retail installment sales	Civil 1801 et seq.
Unfair trade practices	Bus & Prof. 17040 et seq.
Uniform commercial code	Unif. Comm. Code
Usury	Gen. Laws 3757;
	Const. Art. 20, B22
Weights and measures	Bus & Prof. 12001 et seq.

COLORADO (Colorado Revised Statutes, 1963, Supp. 1971)

Advertising	§40-15-1
Collection agencies	27-1-1
Consumer credit code (uniform)	73-1 et seq.
Consumer finance act	73-3-1 et seq.
Consumer protection act	55-5-1 et seq.
Credit unions	38-1-1
False pretenses	40-14-2; 40-5-2
Food	66-20-1 et seq.
Motor vehicle installment sales	13-16-1 et seq.
Uniform commercial code	155-1-101 et seq.
Usury	73-2-7; 73-2-9
Weights and measures	40-14-11; 152-1-1 et seq.

CONNECTICUT (General Statutes of Connecticut, 1958, Supp. 1969)

Consumer advisory council, consumer protection department	§19-170b et seq.
Credit cards	38-380 et seq.
Credit unions	36-194 et seq.
False pretenses	52-360
Finance charge disclosure	36-363
Fraud	53-360 et seq.
Fraudulent conveyances	52-552
Insurance contracts	38-31
Insurance trade practices	38-60 et seq.
Retail installment sales financing	42-83 et seq.; 36-254(o); 52-361(b)
Truth in lending	36-393 et seq.
Unfair sales practices	42-111
Uniform commercial code	42a-1-101 et seq.
Usury	37-4
Weights and measures	43-1 et seq.

DELAWARE (Delaware Code Annotated, 1953, Supp. 1968)

Consumer fraud	Title 6§ 2511 et seq.
Credit cards	11-558
False pretenses	11-554

Food	16-3301 et seq.
Fraudulent conveyances	6-1301 et seq.
Retail installment contracts	5-2901 et seq.
Small loans	5-2101 et seq.
Uniform commercial code	5A-1-101 et seq.
Unsolicited merchandise	6-2505
Usury	6-2301 et seq.
Weights and measures	6-5101 et seq.

FLORIDA (Florida Statutes Annotated, 1963, Supp. 1970)

Consumers advisory council	§20.14
Consumer finance act	519.01 et seq.
Credit cards	817.57 et seq.
Deceptive trade practices	817.69 et seq.
False pretenses	817.01 et seq.
Food	500.01 et seq.
Fraud	817 et seq.
Fraudulent conveyances	726.01 et seq.
Free gift advertising law	817.415
Hazardous substances law	501.061 et seq
Home solicitation sales	501.021 et seq.
Installment land sales	478.211 et seq.
Land contracts, conveyances	689.01 et seq.
Land sales law	478.011 et seq.
Motor vehicle financing	545.01 et seq.
Small loans	516.01 et seq.
Unfair trade practices	817.76 et seq.; 573.17; 573.50; 573.801; 573.857
Uniform commercial code	671.1-101 et seq.
Weights and measures	531.01 et seq.

GEORGIA (Georgia Code Annotated, 1966, Supp. 1970)

(lender) Credit card act	§28-501
Credit card fraud	26-1705.4
Deceptive business practices	26-1706
Food	42-303

Fraud	105-301 et seq.;
	37-701 et seq.
Insurance practices	56-813a; 56-2430
Retail installment sales and	
home solicitation sales act	96-901 et seq.
Uniform commercial code	109A-1-101 et seq.
Uniform deceptive trade practices	106-701 et seq.
Weights and measures	112-9901 et seq.

HAWAII (Hawaii Revised Statutes, 1972)

Collection agencies	§§443-1 et seq.
Consumer counsel	26-7
Credit cards	730-1, 730-12
Food	328-6 et seq.
Fraud	745-1 et seq.;
	747-1 et seq.
Home loans	207-1 et seq.
Land sales act	484-1 et seq.
Peddlers	445-1 et seq.
Retail installment sales	476-1 et seq.
Small loan companies	409-17
Solicitation by telephone	445-184
Truth in lending	477-1 et seq.
Uniform commercial code	490-1-101 et seq.
Usury	478-1 et seq.
Weights and measures	486-1 et seq.

IDAHO (Idaho Code, 1949, Supp. 1970)

Advertising	§18-3112
Collection agencies	26-2222 et seq.
Credit cards	18-3113 et seq.
Credit unions	26-2102; 26-2104;
	26-2116; 26-2124 et seq.
False pretenses	18-3101; 18-3102
Food	37-114
Fraud conspiracy	19-1427
Fraudulent conveyances	55-910 et seq.; 18-3701

Sales frauds	64-603
Small loan act	26-2027 et seq.
Small money lenders act	26-2001 et seq.
Unfair sales act	48-403
Uniform commercial code	Unif. Comm. Code
Usury	27-1906 et seq.
Weights and measures	71-108 et seq.

ILLINOIS (Illinois Annotated Statutes 1961, Supp. 1971)

Advertising	Chap. 121½ §157.21a et seq.
Consumer credit counseling corporation	32-360.1 et seq.
Consumer education courses	122-27-12.1 et seq.
Consumer finance businesses	127-63b35
Consumer finance law	74-19 et seq.
Consumer fraud	121½-261 et seq.
Consumer installment loans	74-51 et seq.
Credit cards	38-17-1; 121½-382
Credit unions	32-496.1 et seq.
Deceptive trade practices	121½-311 et seq.
Food	56½-501 et seq.
Motor vehicle installment sales	121½-502.1; 121½-561 et seq.
Truth in lending	74-4 et seq.
Uniform commercial code	26-1-101 et seq.
Usury	74-70
Warranties, auto	95½-103
Weights and measures	147-101 et seq.

INDIANA (Burns Indiana Statutes, 1954, Supp. 1970) (Citations to the 1971 Indiana Code - "Super Bill" are in parenthesis.)

Advertising	§10-2110 (No Code cite)
Collection practices	10-5007 (35-18-13-1)
Consumer loan act	18-3601 et seq. (28-7-2-1)
Credit cards	10-2130 et seq. (35-18-15-1)
Credit unions	18-2201 et seq. (28-7-1-1)

Food	35-3101 et seq. (16-1-28-1)
Fraudulent conveyances	10-2117 (35-1-116-1); 33-408
Installment loan act	19-2201 et seq. (26-1-2-201);
	19-13-101 et seq. (24-5-4-1)
Retail installment sales act	58-901 et seq. (25-5-2-1)
Uniform commercial code	19-1-101 et seq. (26-1-1-101)
Usury	19-2001 et seq. (No Code cite)
Weights and measures	19-4801 et seq. (35-18-6-1)

IOWA (Iowa Code Annotated, 1951, Supp. 1970)

Advertising	§713.24
Consumer credit loans	554.9203
Consumer fraud	713.24
False pretenses and frauds	713.1 et seq.
Food	191.1 et seq.
Small loans	536.1 et seq.
Uniform commercial code	554.1101 et seq.
Usury	535.4 et seq.
Weights and measures	189.19; 215.6 et seq.

KANSAS (Kansas Statutes Annotated, 1965, Supp. 1969)

Advertising	§21-1102 et seq.
Buyer protection act	50-601 et seq.
Consumer loans	16-401 et seq.
Credit cards	21-589 et seq.
Credit unions	17-2201 et seq.
Food	65-655 et seq.
Fraud	21-561
Installment loans	16-202 et seq.
Retail installment sales	16-501 et seq.
Truth in lending	16-801 et seq.
Uniform commercial code	84-1-101 et seq.
Unsolicited goods	50-617
Usury	16-201 et seq.
Weights and measures	83-101 et seq.

KENTUCKY (Kentucky Revised Statutes, 1969, Supp. 1970)

Advertising	§434.270
Contract against public policy	372.010 et seq.
Credit cards	434.510
Credit unions	290.010 et seq.
Food	217
Fraud	434.010 et seq.
Fraudulent conveyances	378.010 et seq.
Going out of business sale	365.410 et seq.
Installment contracts	371.210 et seq.
Insurance contracts	304.648 et seq.
Interest	360.010 et seq.
Loans, installment	287.215
Motor vehicle installment sales	190.090 et seq.
Peddlers, hawkers, itinerant vendors	84.190; 365.250
Trade practices	365.010 et seq.
Truth in lending	360.210 et seq.
Uniform commercial code	355.1-101 et seq.
Weights and measures	363

LOUISIANA (Louisiana Statutes, 1970)

Advertising	§43:1 et seq.
Collection agencies	47:355
Consumer credit	6:1081 et seq.
Consumer education	33:7501
Contracts	Civil Code II and 1846 and 1863 and 2589
Credit cards	9:3509; 14:67.3
Credit unions	6:641 et seq.
Food	40:601 et seq.
Fraud	6:953; Civil code 1848 and 2547
Fraudulent conveyances	9:2989
Going out of business sale	51:411
Motor vehicle installment sales	6:951

Peddlers	46:371 et seq.;
	33:4832 et seq.;
	47:368 et seq.; 33:401
Small loans	6:571 et seq.
Unfair sales	51:421 et seq.
Usury	Civil code 2924
Weights and measures	55:1 et seq.

MAINE (Maine Revised Statutes, 1964, Supp. 1970)

Advertising	§4-859; 17-1620
Consumer protection (unfair trade)	5-206 et seq.
Credit cards	17-1621 et seq.
Credit unions	9-1 et seq.
Deceptive trade practices	10-1211 et seq.
Food	7-488; 17-3451 et seq.;
	22-2151 et seq.
Fraud	17-1612; 15-753
Fraudulent conveyances	14-6051; 14-2014; 17-1613
Going out of business sale	32-4553
Hazardous substances	7-501 et seq.
Home repair financing	9-3721 et seq.
Home solicitation sales	32-4661 et seq.
Insurance trade practices	24-2901 et seq.
Meat inspection	22-2541 et seq.
Motor vehicle sales finance act	9-3401 et seq.
Packaging and labeling	7-521 et seq.
Peddlers, hawkers; itinerant merchants	32-4501 et seq.
Small loans	9-3001; 9-3041 et seq.
Toys (stuffed)	26-121 et seq.
Truth in lending	9-3801 et seq.
Unfair trade practices	5-206 et seq.
Uniform commercial code	11-1-101 et seq.
Unsolicited merchandise	33-1101
Usury	9-3086
Weights and measures	10-2301 et seq.

MARYLAND (Annotated Code of Maryland, 1970)

Advertising	Art. 27§195 et seq.
	48A-217 et seq.;
	83-146
Consumer protection	83-20 et seq.
Credit unions	11-135 et seq.
Fair trade	83-102 et seq.
Food	43-175 et seq.
Fraud	27-159 et seq.
Fraudulent conveyances	39B-1 et seq.
Home improvements	56-250 et seq.
Installment sales	83-128 et seq.
Labeling	66C-470c; 43-187; 27-274;
	43-165
Motor vehicle installment sales	83-132
Peddlers	56-21 et seq.
Pesticides	48-129 et seq.
Retail credit accounts	83-153A et seq.
Small loans	58A-1 et seq.
Trading stamps	56-21 et seq.
Uniform commercial code	95B-1-101 et seq.
Weights and measures	97

MASSACHUSETTS (Annotated Laws of Massachusetts, 1962, Supp. 1970)

Advertising	Chap. 266§89 et seq.
Collections	41-38A; 99-1 et seq.
Consumers Council	6A-9
Consumer protection (unfair trade)	93A-1 et seq.
Containers	94-99B; 94-181
Credit bureaus	93-44 et seq.
Credit cards	140C:6(d); 266-37A;
	255-12
Credit unions	171-1 et seq.
False pretenses	266-30 et seq.
Food	94-186 et seq.
Fraud	266-76; 277-30
Fraudulent conveyances	109A-1 et seq.

Unsolicited merchandise	19.416
Weights and measures	12.1081 et seq.

MINNESOTA (Minnesota Statutes 1962; Supp. 1971)

Advertising	§325.905; 184.15; 620.52
Collection agencies	332.01 et seq.
Consumer fraud	325.78 et seq.
Consumer services office	45.15 et seq.
Credit cards	325.93 et seq.; 609.52; 622.28; 62.501
Credit unions	52.01 et seq.
False pretenses	613.70; 620.50; 622.14; 620.47; 626.01
Food	31.01 et seq.
Fraud	513.01 et seq.
Fraudulent conveyances	513.08 et seq.
Hazardous substances	24.32 et seq.
Insurance practices	72A-17 et seq.
Labeling	620.26; 620.27; 620.55; 325.05; 31A.02
Motor vehicle retail installment sales	168.66 et seq.
Peddlers	329.02
Small loans	56.01 et seq.
Unfair trade practices	325.01 et seq.
Uniform commercial code	336.1-101 et seq.
Unsolicited goods	325.92
Usury	334.01 et seq.
Weights and measures	239.01 et seq.

MISSISSIPPI (Mississippi Code, 1958, Supp. 1970)

Advertising	§2003.5; 2144.3; 5591-05
Closing - out sales	5152-01 et seq.
Credit cards	2148.5 et seq.
Credit unions	5391 et seq.

False pretenses	2145 et seq.
Food	7107 et seq.
Fraudulent conveyances	265 et seq.
Installment sales	892; 875
Insurances practices	5649-04
Meat inspection	4575 et seq.
Motor vehicle sales	8075 et seq.
Peddlers	3374-131
Small loans	5212; 5591 et seq.
Toys	3374-124; 2319
Trading stamps	4560-107(b); 9696-183; 4560-156 et seq.
Unfair trade practices	4560-107
Uniform commercial code	41A:1-101 et seq.
Usury	5359-53; 5288-15(b)
Weights and measures	5132-01 et seq.

MISSOURI (Missouri Statutes, 1953, Supp. 1970)

Advertising	§ 561.660; 561.665; 408.160
Consumer credit loans	367.100 et seq.; 59.163
Credit unions	370
False pretenses	454.180 et seq.
Food	400.2-314; 196; 265.370
Fraud	561
Fraudulent conveyances	428
Insurance practices	375.930 et seq.
Motor vehicle time sales	365.010 et seq.
Peddlers, itinerant vendors, hawkers	150.420; 150; 73.110; 75.110; 94.110; 94.270; 94.360; 80.090
Small loans	408.175; 367.100; 408.200
Toys	75.110
Unfair trade practices	407.010 et seq.
Uniform commercial code	400.1-101 et seq.

Unsolicited merchandise	407.200
Usury	408.050 et seq.; 561.430
Weights and measures	413.225 et seq.

MONTANA (Revised Codes of Montana, 1957, Supp. 1969)

Advertising	§47-219; 94-1818 et seq.
Consumer loan act	47-201 et seq.
Contracts	13-302; 13-903 et seq; 17-902 et seq.
Credit cards	94-1823 et seq.
Credit unions	14-130 et seq.
Food	27-705 et seq.
Fraud	94-1801 et seq.; 94-1901 et seq.
Fraudulent conveyances	94-2101 et seq.
Installment sales act	74-601 et seq.
Insurance practices	40-905
Interest	47-124
Uniform commercial code	87A-1-101 et seq.
Unsolicited goods	67-1706.1
Weights and measures	90-101 et seq.; 94-1901 et seq.

NEBRASKA (Revised Statutes of Nebraksa, 1969, Supp. 1970)

Advertising	§28-1235 et seq.
Collection agencies	81-8; 158
Credit cards	28-1240 et seq.
Credit unions	21-1760 et seq.
Dairy industry trade practices	81-263.37 et seq.
Deceptive trade practices	87-301 et seq.
False pretenses	28-1207
Food	81-217.11 et seq.
Fraud	28-1223; 28-301; 69-1214; 45-350; 28-445
Fraudulent conveyances	76-201 et seq.; 36-101 et seq.
Installment sales	45-334 et seq.
Insurance practices	44-501 et seq.

Peddlers	75-323 et seq.
Uniform commercial code	Unif. Comm. Code
Unsolicited goods	63-104
Usury	45-101
Weights and measures	89-101 et seq.

NEVADA (Nevada Revised Statutes, 1971)

Advertising	§207.170; 585.520
Collection agencies	649.051 et seq.
Credit cards	205.500
Food	585.230 et seq.
Fraud	205.330 et seq.
Fraudulent conveyances	112.010 et seq.
Fraudulent practices	686.400 et seq.
Insurance practices	686.390 et seq.
Labeling - agricultural products	587.460 et seq.
Land sales	119.010 et seq.
Peddlers	650.010 et seq.
Retail installment sales	97.015 et seq.
Sales; pyramid promotional	598.100 et seq.
Small loans	675.010 et seq.
Trade practices	598.030; 584.570; 482.3631
Trading stamps	639.215
Uniform commercial code	104.1101 et seq.
Unit pricing	581.303
Unsolicited merchandise	598.090
Usury	99.050
Weights and measures	581.001 et seq.

NEW HAMPSHIRE (New Hampshire Revised Statutes, 1955, Supp. 1969)

Advertising	§580:9
Credit cards	580:9a et seq.; 402:15-a
Credit unions	394:1 et seq.
Deceptive practices	358-A:1 et seq.
False pretenses	580:1

NEW JERSEY (New Jersey Statutes, 1957, Supp. 1970)

Weights and measures	51:1-1 et seq.

NEW MEXICO (New Mexico Statutes, 1965, Supp. 1969)

Advertising	§67-15-77; 49-1-5; 54-1-3
Collection agencies	67-15-22 et seq.
Credit bureaus	50-18-2 et seq.
Credit cards	50-19-1; 40A-16-24 et seq.
Credit unions	48-19-1 et seq.
Food	54-1-1 et seq.
Fraud	40A-16-6; 76-1-40; 76-1-41; 76-1-53
Fraudulent conveyances	50-14-1 et seq.
Installment loans	48-21-1 et seq.
Installment sales	50-16-1 et seq.
Insurance practices	58-9-11 et seq.
Meat inspection	54-8-6 et seq.
Peddlers	60-2-1 et seq.
Trading stamps	49-9-1 et seq.
Uniform commercial code	50-A-1-101 et seq.
Usury	50-6-3 et seq.
Weights and measures	14-17-10; 76-1-28 et seq.

NEW YORK (Consolidated Laws of New York, 1968, Supp. 1970)

Advertising	
false	Gen. Bus 350 et seq.
food	Agric. & M 202-a
loans	Penal 190.20
Collection agencies	Penal 190.50; Judic 489; Gen. Bus 84
Consumer protection board	Exec 550 et seq.
Credit cards	Gen. Bus 511 et seq.
Credit information	Gen. Bus 370 et seq.
Credit unions	Bank 450 et seq.
Deceptive practices	Gen. Bus 349 et seq.
Fine art, warranties	Gen. Bus 221 et seq.

Food

NORTH CAROLINA (General Statutes of North Carolina, 1962, Supp. 1969)

| Usury | 24-1 et seq.; 14-391 |
| Weights and measures | 81-1 et seq. |

NORTH DAKOTA (North Dakota Century Code, 1960, Supp. 1969)

Advertising	§51-12-01 et seq.
Collection agencies	13-05-01 et seq.
Contracts	9-09-02 et seq.
Credit cards	51-14.1-01
Credit unions	6-06-01 et seq.
Food	19-02-02 et seq.;
	19-02.1-01 et seq.
Fraud	9-03-05 et seq.
Fraudulent conveyances	13-02-01 et seq.
Installment loans	13-04-01 et seq.
Installment sales	51-13-02 et seq.
Insurance contracts	26-02-01 et seq.
Insurance practices	26-30-01 et seq.
Loans	13-03-01 et seq.;
	47-14-01 et seq.
Meat inspection	36-23.1-01 et seq.
Retail sales protection	51-15-01 et seq.;
	51-10-14 et seq.
Transient merchants	51-04-01 et seq.; 40-05-01
Uniform commercial code	41-01-01 et seq.
Usury	47-14-05 et seq.
Weights and measures	64-01-01 et seq.

OHIO (Ohio Revised Code, 1967, Supp. 1970)

Advertising	§2911.41 et seq.; 3923.16;
	3999.10 et seq.
Collecting banks	1304.01 et seq.
Credit cards	1319.01; 2907.20.1(A) et seq.
Credit unions	1733.03 et seq.
Deceptive trade practices	4165.01 et seq.

False pretenses	2907.30; 2911.01
Food	3715.01 et seq.
Fraud	3999.01; 3599.42
Fraudulent conveyances	1336.01 et seq.
Hazardous substances	3716.01 et seq.
Insurance practices	3901.19 et seq.
Labeling, packaging	925.21 et seq.; 1327.44; 3715.14 et seq.
Motor vehicle installment contracts	4517.14 et seq.
Peddlers	715.61 et seq.
Retail installment sales	1317.01 et seq.
Small loans	1321.01 et seq.
Toys	3713.01 et seq.
Trading stamps	1333.01 et seq.
Uniform commercial code	1301.01 et seq.
Usury	1321.13; 1115.10; 1115.21
Weights and measures	1327.01 et seq.

OKLAHOMA (Oklahoma Statutes, 1956, Supp. 1970)

Advertising	§21-1502; 63-180.2 et seq.
Collection by banks	6-118 et seq.
Consumer credit code	14A-1-101 et seq.
Contracts	15-232 et seq.
Credit agencies, ratings	24-81 et seq.
Credit cards	21-1550.2 et seq.
Credit unions	6-375.1 et seq.
Fair trade act	78-41 et seq.
False pretenses	21-1541 et seq.
Food	63-180.1 et seq.
Fraud	21-1501 et seq.
Fraudulent conveyances	21-1671 et seq.; 24-5-11 et seq.
Hazardous substances	63-1-1601 et seq.
Insurance practices	36-149; 36-117.1 et seq.

Motor vehicle sales	47-569 et seq.
Peddlers, hawkers, itinerant vendors	11-651; 11-1005; 47-434; 59-515; 63-201
Trading stamps	21-361 et seq.
Uniform commercial code	12A-1-101 et seq.
Unsolicited goods	15-721 et seq.
Usury	Const. 14-2; 15-267 et seq.
Weights and measures	83-1 et seq.

OREGON (Oregon Revised Statutes, 1969)

Advertising	§59.260; 698.640; 646.810; 646.990
Collection agency	697.010 et seq.
Credit cards	165.290; 165.615
Credit unions	723.010 et seq.
False pretenses	165.205; 165.265
Food	616.010 et seq.
Fraud	165 et seq.
Insurance policies	743.003 et seq.
Peddlers	670.220 et seq.
Retail installment contracts	83.010 et seq.
Trade practices	746.005 et seq.
Uniform commercial code	71.1010 et seq.
Unsolicited goods	98.450
Usury	82.010 et seq.
Weights and measures	618.010 et seq.

PENNSYLVANIA (Pennsylvania Statutes, 1959, Supp. 1970)

Advertising	§31-800-1; 18-4857; 53-4471-1 et seq.
Collection agencies	18-4895
Consumer discount companies	7-761-1 et seq.
Consumer protection	73-201-1 et seq.
Credit life insurance	40-1007.1 et seq.

Credit unions	15-12301 et seq.;
	14-201 et seq.
Fair trade act	73-1 et seq.
Food	18-4635; 31-1 et seq.
Fraud	19-331; 18-4302;
	18-4851.1; 19-981
Fraudulent conveyances	39-351 et seq.
Hazardous substances	75-2401 et seq.
Home improvement finance act	73-500-101 et seq.
Installment sales	69-1101 et seq.
Insurance practices	40-1151 et seq.
Meat	31-461 et seq.
Motor vehicle sales finance	69-601 et seq.
Peddlers	53-37601; 60-1 et. seq.
Small loan act	7-751 et seq.
Unfair trade practices	73-201-1 et seq.
Uniform commercial code	12A-1-101 et seq.
Unsolicited merchandise	73-2001
Usury	41-2 et seq.
Weights and measures	76-1 et seq.

RHODE ISLAND (General Laws of Rhode Island, 1958, Supp. 1970)

Advertising	§21-31-3; 11-18-10 et seq.
Consumers co-operatives	7-8-1 et seq.
Consumers council	42-42-1 et seq.
Credit cards	11-49-1 et seq.
Credit insurance	27-31-2 et seq.
Credit unions	19-21-1 et seq.
Deceptive trade practices	6-13.1-1 et seq.
Food	21-1-1 et seq.
Fraud	47-3-3; 11-18-10 et seq.
Fraudulent conveyances	6-16-1 et seq.
Insurance trade practices	27-29-1 et seq.
Peddlers	5-11-1 et seq.
Small loans	19-25-1 et seq.

Trading stamps	11-19-9 et seq.
Truth in lending	6-27-1 et seq.
Uniform commercial code	6A-1-101 et seq.
Usury	6-26-1 et seq.
Weights and measures	47-15-1 et seq.

SOUTH DAKOTA (South Dakota Compiled Laws, 1967, Supp. 1970)

Advertising	§22-41-10 et seq.
Collection agencies	54-4-10
Consumer affairs office	37-23-1 et seq.
Contracts	53-11-1 et seq.
Credit cards	54-11-1 et seq.
Credit insurance	58-19-1 et seq.
Fair trade	37-9-1 et seq.
False pretenses	23-44-13; 22-41-4 et seq.
Food	39-1 et seq.
Fraud	20-10-2
Fraudulent conveyances	54-8-1 et seq.
Installment loans	54-4-1 et seq.
Insurance practices	58-33-1 et seq.
Motor vehicle installment sales	54-7-1 et seq.
Solicitors	37-13-1 et seq.
Uniform commercial code	57-1-1 et seq.
Usury	54-3-1 et seq.
Weights and measures	

TENNESSEE (Tennessee Code Annotated, 1956, Supp. 1970)

Advertising	§39-1911; 56-1204; 45-2112; 52-917; 62-1101 et seq.; 69-601 et seq.
Closing out sales	6-714 et seq.
Collection agencies	67-4203
Credit cards	39-1968 et seq.
Credit unions	45-1801 et seq.

Fair trade	69-201 et seq.
False pretenses	39-1945; 39-1901 et seq.
Food	52-101 et seq.
Fraud	39-1901 et seq.
Fraudulent conveyance	64-308 et seq.
Hazardous substances	53-3701 et seq.
Insurance practices	56-1201 et seq.
Labeling	71-233; 52-304; 52-917; 71-223
Loans	45-2101 et seq.
Motor vehicle financing	59-1301 et seq.
Peddlers, transient merchants	67-4601 et seq.; 67-4801 et seq.
Retail installment sales	47-11-101 et seq.
Trading stamps	67-4203 item 106
Truth in lending	47-14-119
Unfair practices	
frozen desserts	52-335 et seq.
household goods	69-601 et seq.
milk products	52-331 et seq.
Uniform commercial code	47-1-101 et seq.
Usury	47-14-104; 47-14-112 et seq.
Weights and measures	71-201 et seq.

TEXAS (Texas Statutes, 1958, Supp. 1971)
(references are to civil statutes unless otherwise indicated)

Advertising	Penal 1554
Consumer credit	Art. 5069-2.01 et seq.
Consumer protection (unfair trade)	5069-9.01 et seq.
Credit cards	Penal 1155b; Penal 1555c; Penal 1137e-1
Credit insurance	5069-3.18; 5069-4.02
Credit unions	2461 et seq.
Deceptive practices	5069-10.01 et seq.
False pretenses	Penal 1545
Food	4465a et seq.

Trading stamps	13-6-1 et seq.
Unfair trade practices	13-5-1 et seq.
Uniform commercial code	70A-1-101 et seq.
Usury	15-1-1
Weights and measures	5-6-1 et seq.

VERMONT (Vermont Statutes, 1959, Supp. 1970)

Advertising	Title 13§ 2005; 18-4068; 9-2452
Consumer fraud	9-2451 et seq.
Credit cards	9-404 et seq.
Credit unions	8-1731 et seq.; 8-2051
False pretenses	13-2002
Food	18-4051 et seq.; 18-4001 et seq.
Fraud	13-2010 et seq.
Fraudulent conveyances	9-2281
Hazardous substances	18-4051 et seq.
Insurance practices	8-4721 et seq.
Interest	9-41 et seq.
Labeling	6-3201; 18-4051
Motor vehicle financing	9-2351 et seq.
Peddlers, vendors	32-9301 et seq.; 32-9201 et seq.
Retail installment sales	9-2401 et seq.
Small loans	8-3001 et seq.
Trading stamps	9-4021 et seq.
Uniform commercial code	9A-1-101 et seq.
Weights and measures	9-2631 et seq.

VIRGINIA (Code of Virginia, 1963, Supp. 1970)

Advertising	§59.1-45; 54-815; 3-306; 38.1-52
Collection agencies	18.1-406; 54-729.1 et seq.
Consumer affairs counsel	2.1-133.1 et seq.
Consumer credit	6.1-352 et seq.
Correspondence schools	22-330.17 et seq.
Credit cards	11-30 et seq.; 18.1-119 et seq.
Credit unions	6-202 et seq.; 6.1-196

Fair trade practices	59.1-1 et seq.
False pretenses	18.1-118 et seq.; 59.1-45
Food	3-306 et seq.; 3.1-386 et seq.
Fraud	63-217; 18.1-116; 6.1-280
Fraudulent conveyances	55-80 et seq.
Hazardous substances	3.1-250 et seq.
Home solicitation sales	59.1-21.1 et seq.
Insurance practices	38.1-49 et seq.
Motor vehicle financing	46.1-516 et seq.
Packaging, labeling	59.1-93 et seq.
Peddlers	58-340; 54-809 et seq.
Small loans	6.1-244 et seq.
Uniform commercial code	8.1-101 et seq.
Usury	6.1-319.1 et seq.
Weights and measures	3-708.1 et seq.

WASHINGTON (Revised Code of Washington, 1965, Supp. 1972)

Advertising	§9.04; 69.04; 710
Collection agencies	19.16.110
Consumer protection act	19.86
Credit cards	9.26A.010 et seq.
Credit insurance	48.34
Credit unions	31.12
Employment agencies	19.31
False pretenses	9.37
Food	69.04 et seq.
Franchise investment protection act	19.100.010
Fraud	9.45; 9.38; 9.22
Fraudulent conveyances	19.40
Insurance practices	48.30
Motor vehicle financing	46.76.130

Packaging, labeling	69.04.013; 69.04.015; 69.04.050; 15.36.011; 69.04.333; 16.49A.300; 9.16.010
Peddlers	36.71; 45.12.100; 35.23.440
Retail installment sales	63.14
Small loans	31.08
Trading stamps	19.84
Unfair trade	19.89; 19.90
Uniform commercial code	621.1-101 et seq.
Unsolicited goods	19.56
Usury	19.52
Weights and measures	19.92; 19.33

WEST VIRGINIA (West Virginia Code, 1966, Supp. 1970)

Advertising	§61-3-38
Collection agencies	11-12-12
Credit cards	61-3-24a
Credit unions	31-10
False pretenses	61-3
Food	16-7
Fraud	61-3-40; 55-2-7
Fraudulent conveyances	40-1-1 et seq.
Insurance practices	33-11
Labeling	47-1-24
Peddlers	11-12-8
Small loans	47-7A-1 et seq.
Trading stamps	11-12-5
Unfair trade	47-11
Uniform commercial code	46-1-101 et seq.
Unsolicited goods	47-11A-12a
Usury	47-6-5 et seq.
Weights and measures	47-1

WISCONSIN (Wisconsin Statutes Annotated, 1958, Supp. 1970)

Advertising	§100.18; 97.64; 214.16

Appendix B

CREDIT SALE CONTRACT — Reg. §226.8(a),(c)

$\overline{\qquad}$ $\overline{\qquad}$
(City)   (State)

_____ 19___

The undersigned Seller agrees to sell and the undersigned Buyers, jointly and severally, agree to purchase the following goods on the following terms:

Description of goods . . . .

Statement of Transaction

1. **CASH PRICE** . . . . **$_____**

2. **LESS DOWNPAYMENT:**
   a. CASH DOWNPAYMENT . . . . $_____
   b. TRADE-IN . . . . $_____
   TOTAL DOWNPAYMENT . . . . **$_____**

3. **UNPAID BALANCE OF CASH PRICE (item 1 minus item 2)** . . . . **$_____**

4. **OTHER CHARGES:**
   a. _____ . . . . $_____
   b. _____ . . . . $_____
   OTHER CHARGES . . . . **$_____**

5. **AMOUNT FINANCED (items 3 and 4)** . . . . **$_____**

6. **FINANCE CHARGE:**
   a. _____ . . . . $_____
   b. _____ . . . . $_____
   c. _____ . . . . $_____
   FINANCE CHARGE . . . . **$_____**

7. **ANNUAL PERCENTAGE RATE** . . . . _____ %

8. **TOTAL OF PAYMENTS (items 5 and 6)** . . . . **$_____**

9. **DEFERRED PAYMENT PRICE (items 2 and 7)** . . . . **$_____**

10. Payment schedule: _____ consecutive monthly payments of $_____ each beginning one month from the date hereof and thereafter on the same date of each subsequent month until paid in full.

11. Buyers agree to pay Seller at above place. All or part of unpaid balance may be paid, at any time, without penalty, and any unearned finance charge will be refunded based on the "Rule of 78's." Seller agrees to deliver conforming goods on execution of contract. If Seller fails to deliver within 30 days, Buyers may rescind contract. If Buyers fail to pay an instalment within 30 after it is due, a charge of _____ may be assessed.

Buyers _____

_____

_____

Seller _____

DISCLOSURES
CREDIT SALE CONTRACT* – Reg. §226.8(a),(c)

Seller's Name: _____   Contract #_____

RETAIL INSTALLMENT CONTRACT AND SECURITY AGREEMENT

The undersigned (herein called Purchaser, whether one or more) purchases from _____ (seller) and grants to _____ a security interest in, subject to the terms and conditions hereof, the following described property.

QUANTITY	DESCRIPTION	AMOUNT	

Description of Trade-In:

	Sales Tax		
	Total		

Insurance Agreement

The purchase of insurance coverage is voluntary and not required for credit.   (Type of Ins.)
Insurance coverage is available at a cost of $_____ for the term of credit.

I desire insurance coverage

Signed_____ Date_____

I do not desire insurance coverage

Signed_____ Date_____

PURCHASER'S NAME_____
PURCHASER'S ADDRESS_____
CITY_____ STATE_____ ZIP_____

1. CASH PRICE	$_____	
2. LESS: CASH DOWN PAYMENT	$_____	
3. TRADE-IN	_____	
4. TOTAL DOWN PAYMENT	_____ $	
5. UNPAID BALANCE OF CASH PRICE	$_____	
6. OTHER CHARGES:		
_____	$_____	
_____	_____	
7. AMOUNT FINANCED	$_____	
8. FINANCE CHARGE	$_____	
9. TOTAL OF PAYMENTS	$_____	
10. DEFERRED PAYMENT PRICE (1+6+8)	$_____	
11. ANNUAL PERCENTAGE RATE	_____%	

Purchaser hereby agrees to pay to_____
_____ at their offices shown above the "TOTAL OF PAYMENTS" shown above in _____ monthly installments of $_____ (final payment to be $_____) the first installment being payable _____ 19_____, and all subsequent installments on the same day of each consecutive month until paid in full. The finance charge applies from ____(Date)

Signed_____

Notice to Buyer: You are entitled to a copy of the contract you sign. You have the right to pay in advance the unpaid balance of this contract and obtain a partial refund of the finance charge based on the "Actuarial Method." [Any other method of computation may be so identified, for example, "Rule of 78's," "Sum of the Digits," etc.]

*Source: What you ought to know about Federal Reserve Regulation Z, Exhibit C, p. 22 (Washington, D.C.: Board of Governors of the Federal Reserve System, 1969)

INSTALMENT LOAN CONTRACT — Reg. § 226.8(a), (d)

_____   _____
(City)   (State)

_____ 19____

The undersigned makers, jointly and severally, promise to pay to_____
_____ at the above place_____ dollars ($____)
in_____ consecutive monthly payments of $_____, each beginning one month
from the date hereof and thereafter on the same date of each subsequent month until
paid in full. Any unpaid balance may be paid, at any time, without penalty and any
unearned finance charge will be refunded based on the "Rule of 78's." In the event
that makers default for more than 30 days in any payment, a charge of_____may be
assessed.

1. AMOUNT FINANCED.

     a. _____ $_____
     b. _____ $_____
     c. _____ $_____
     d. _____ $_____
     AMOUNT FINANCED (items a through d) . . . . $_____

2. FINANCE CHARGE.

     a. _____ $_____
     b. _____ $_____
     c. _____ $_____
     d. _____ $_____
     FINANCE CHARGE (items a through d). . . . . $_____

3. TOTAL OF PAYMENTS (items 1 and 2) . . . . $_____

4. TOTAL PREPAID FINANCE CHARGE AND REQUIRED DEPOSIT BALANCE.

     a. PREPAID FINANCE CHARGE . . . . $_____
     b. REQUIRED DEPOSIT BALANCE . . . . $_____
     TOTAL PREPAID FINANCE CHARGE
     AND REQUIRED DEPOSIT BALANCE . . . . $_____

5. ANNUAL PERCENTAGE RATE . . . . _____%

Signed_____

Form 1310

Example of disclosures on a promissory note for non-sale credit for which a finance charge is added to the amount financed and the obligation is repayable in installments.

PROMISSORY NOTE

_____, _____
(City)   (State)

_____19____

For value received, undersigned maker(s), jointly and severally, promise to pay to the order of _____ at the above place _____ dollars ($_____) in _____ consecutive monthly payments of $_____, each beginning one month from the date hereof and thereafter on the same date of each subsequent month until paid in full. Any unpaid balance may be paid, at any time, without penalty and any unearned finance charge will be refunded based on the "Rule of 78's". In the event that maker(s) default(s) on any payment, a charge of _____ may be assessed.

1. Proceeds $_____

2. _____   _____
   (Other charges, Itemized)
3. Amount financed (1+2) $_____

4. FINANCE CHARGE   _____

5. Total of payments $_____
   ANNUAL PERCENTAGE RATE   _____ %

Signed _____

_____

_____

---

*Source: What you ought to know about Federal Reserve Regulation Z, Exhibit D, p. 24 (Washington, D.C.: Board of Governors of the Federal Reserve System, 1969)

INDEX